Student Diagnosis, Placement, and Prescription

Student Diagnosis, Placement, and Prescription

A CRITERION-REFERENCED APPROACH

Roger B. Worner

INDIANA UNIVERSITY PRESS • BLOOMINGTON & LONDON

Published in Canada by Fitzhenry & Whiteside Limited, Don Mills, Ontario

Manufactured in the United States of America

Library of Congress Cataloging in Publication Data
Worner, Roger B 1943–
Student diagnosis, placement, and prescription.
1. Students, Rating of. 2. Ability grouping in education. 3. Educational accountability. I. Title.
LB3061.W67   371.2'5   76-26432
ISBN 0-253-35526-5   1 2 3 4 5 81 80 79 78 77

To My Mother and Father

CONTENTS

Preface

In the past decade and, more particularly, during the past five years, an increasing number of educational authors have been addressing facets of diagnosis, placement, and prescription from a criterion-referenced framework. Normally, then, there would be reduced motivation to rework this issue, particularly if earlier works proved to be fairly comprehensive. However, I was struck by three observations typical of educational writing and writers when I reviewed existing works on criterion-referenced approaches.

First, the majority of books and articles addressing generalized diagnostic, placement, and prescriptive approaches from a criterion-referenced vantage point are written by university staff members who frequently employ a language that is difficult to translate and, in addition, they fail to address issues of design and implementation that are so critical to school personnel. Second, many of the works suggest that most school systems are further advanced in developmental activities that would play a part in student diagnosis, placement, and prescription design than they really are. For example, it is often assumed that program skills, concepts, processes, and objectives are fairly well refined in school systems and diagnostic capacities are advanced when, many times, school systems have done nothing in those areas. As a consequence, those authors who have failed to address those issues have started their readers at mid-stream too many times and caused frustration or failure in the design of improved systems and services for students. Third, much of what has been written about student diagnosis, placement, and prescription processes is incomplete or simplified to a point where to design such processes would be to court failure or chaos for the teacher who must make the process work. For example, a suggested design that addresses the issue of improved diagnosis but provides no mechanism for subsequent placement and prescription frustrates school administrators, overwhelms teachers, and potentially misinforms the public.

In light of those observations, I have developed a criterion-referenced approach to student diagnosis, placement, and prescription that would be understandable, complete, and could be designed in either a simple or complex fashion. The first part of each chapter deals with an approach that could be employed by a school system in its design work. Near the end of each chapter is a section treating design work that could be undertaken by the classroom teacher if the school system were not predisposed to develop a systemic diagnostic, placement, and prescriptive process. Each chapter provides some form of definition, the values of the component discussed in the chapter, the design of the component discussed, design work for the teacher, and select documents appropriated from school systems employing a diagnostic, placement, and prescriptive approach to student instruction.

After the first introductory chapter, the book treats the major components of the process: the instructional program foundation, diagnosis, placement, and prescription. The final chapter illustrates through an actual case study the integration of a criterion-referenced approach to student diagnosis, placement, and prescription.

One should note that the book's underlying intent is to *increase* teacher and student options in the teaching-learning process—not to reduce them. It is all too often assumed that in order to specify and develop curricular processes and programs one must make them inflexible and unimaginative. The process suggested in this book is intended to increase a school system's and teacher's proficiency and speed in effectively carrying out diagnosis, placement, prescription, assessment, and supplementation according to programs that are locally conceived. Such a process does not suggest that those locally conceived programs be unimaginative, but it does require that they be clearly and representatively stated and able to have diagnostic, placement, and prescriptive devices constructed against them. Within this frame of reference, teachers should have the latitude to conceive methodological and material resources that they feel will best serve the students' needs from among those available in the school system.

Acknowledgments are offered to a number of individuals who assisted the author in the completion of this book. Above all else, the author is indebted to his wife, Merida, for her patience in keeping him at his self-appointed task and her critical review and comment on every facet of this work. Further, the author acknowledges his two brothers: Dr. Wayne Worner, Head, Division of Administration and Supervision, Virginia Polytechnic Institute and State University, Blacksburg, Virginia and Dr. Mike Worner, Director of Instruction, Bensenville Public Schools, Bensenville, Illinois, who as knowledgeable educators and constructive critics of educational processes, have served as a sounding board for ideas contained in the work.

A special debt of gratitude is expressed to Dr. Cathy Candor, Director of Research and Evaluation, Kanawha County Schools, Charleston, West Virginia for her capable assistance in the third chapter of the book and, also, for her outstanding and pragmatic work with diagnostic and placement design work in the Kanawha County Schools.

Thanks are tendered to the following school systems and their teachers and administrators for giving the author an opportunity to work with them in their design of criterion-referenced approaches to student diagnosis, placement, and prescription: Fargo Public Schools, Fargo, North Dakota; Kanawha County Schools, Charleston, West Virginia; Libertyville Public Schools, Libertyville, Illinois; Roanoke City Public Schools, Roanoke, Virginia; Tinley Park Public Schools, Tinley Park, Illinois; and West Northfield Public Schools, Northbrook, Illinois.

Finally, Mrs. Lynn Miller, the author's secretary, at the Institute for Educational Research, is recognized for her stalwart efforts in editing and typing the manuscript for submission to the publisher.

Roger B. Worner
Chicago 1977

Student Diagnosis, Placement, and Prescription

1. The Realm of School System Instruction

Mary Jane Andrews arrived early for the appointment with her son's teacher at Robins Elementary School. It was the fourth such meeting this school year, and it was barely mid-December. While waiting for Miss Johnson, Jared's teacher, to arrive, Mrs. Andrews felt the red burn of disgust creep into her cheeks. She and her husband Todd had been through this drama often enough to know that there would be a rehash of "Jared's problems," so fully disclosed on the three previous occasions. How she hated the prospect of hearing again about "Jared's lack of interest, sullen attitude, and poor performance." "He shouldn't have problems," the teacher had told them, "he comes from a good family where learning is obviously valued." The comment undoubtedly referred to the fact that both of the Andrews were college graduates and that Todd Andrews was an exceedingly successful local attorney. Nonetheless, Jared was having problems.

What annoyed the Andrews at each conference was the failure of the principal or teacher to suggest any course of action for solving Jared's poor school performance. With each encounter the Andrews had asked what they could do. They were told again and again that they should "bear down harder on Jared and make him assume more responsibility." This, the Andrews now felt, was not the solution. They had tried to work with him on his classwork but felt there was a practical limitation on how much they could do and how many after-school and evening study sessions should be imposed upon a third grade child. Because he was somewhat shy and withdrawn anyway, they were fearful that he was becoming even more so as they continued to pressure him to perform. Over the past few months conditions had degenerated to the point where Jared exclaimed that he hated school, and he frequently "lost" worksheets completed in school, "forgot" his books, and claimed that his teacher had made no assignment for the next day.

Though he had never been a bright child, Jared had always been an average performer in school. In his first three years of formal schooling at Taft Elementary School, he occasionally had a few B's and nearly all C's on his report card. He liked school and his teachers, and they were fond of him. All of this changed when the family moved across town to Robins Elementary where, according to Principal Pete Edwards, "Things are done differently than at old Taft Elementary!" The children were brighter at Robins, and the reading and mathematics programs were much more abstract and, supposedly, accelerated. Mr. Edwards had told the Andrews at the parent orientation session that Jared would probably find Robins Elementary to be "quite demanding" because of the type of student clientele at the school and the stringent school and teacher standards maintained. He was right. Jared did have a tough time of it. He did not adjust to the mathematics programs at Robins, and almost from the first day in his new setting, his reading ability deteriorated.

At their first conference, the teacher showed the Andrews Jared's standardized test results that "proved he should be able to do average third grade work," but, she noted, "he does have some weaknesses we'll have to work on." There was no elaboration on the weaknesses until the second conference when the Andrews learned that their son would be placed in a different reading and mathematics group with different books because of "some skill weaknesses." By the time the third conference was completed the teacher said she was confused about Jared because "he should be able to perform, but he isn't." On that occasion there was some mention of further testing and possibly having the remedial reading teacher see Jared. The teacher commented that Jared obviously had had inferior instruction at Taft because he couldn't handle the basic subjects at Robins. She further hypothesized with the Andrews that "it is possible Jared was not really as good a student as the Taft teachers informed us. Perhaps he really should be grouped with second grade children in reading and math." When Todd Andrews asked about the standardized test results he had seen earlier that showed Jared's ability to do third grade work, she quickly dismissed the test saying, "Oh, they only give part of the picture. In fact they are often inaccurate with some children." The conference ended without any direction for how the Andrews should proceed with Jared's instruction or a clear specification of his problems and the course of action the school intended to take. The teacher and principal simply indicated that they would "get in touch if something new developed." Presumably things had developed, and a fourth meeting was scheduled.

Deeply engrossed in these thoughts, Mrs. Andrews barely noticed the door of the conference room open as Jared's teacher entered. Miss Johnson greeted Mary Jane warmly and exchanged a few pleasantries.

"This past week," she said, "Jared has really begun to give me problems in class. As you may be aware, the second grade teacher, Mrs. Phillips, and I agreed to have Jared attend a reading group in the second grade during the regular language arts block. Well, Jared's giving us a rough time of it. It seems he dislikes reading with little kids, and he refuses to read at all."

"I wasn't aware that . . . . ," interjected Mrs. Andrews, only to be cut short.

"Frankly we feel we've done just about everything we can with him. We'll continue to work, but we are going to need a lot of support from you and your husband!"

"In what way?" asked Mrs. Andrews.

"Well, for one thing, Jared has been getting quite unruly in class—refusing to do his work or read out loud in class. I nearly sent him out of class."

"Do you think that would help him learn how to read?"

"Well, I don't know that it really would, but it would certainly help him to understand that we mean to have learning take place here at Robins. And, personally, I will not tolerate . . ." said Miss Johnson before being interrupted.

"I'm glad you mentioned that you wanted learning to take place at Robins. That's exactly what Mr. Andrews and I want to take place. In our estimation, however, Jared isn't learning much of anything. Can you explain that to us? You haven't in the past three conferences we've had with you."

"Just a minute now, Mrs. Andrews, Jared does have some specific learning problems that are not easily overcome, but we are taking the actions we feel are best for him."

"What are Jared's *specific* learning problems and what are you doing about them?" asked Mrs. Andrews.

"He is unable to read as well as his third grade peers and not able to keep up on his assignments. We've placed him with second grade children in reading and mathematics," explained Miss Johnson.

"But he's already completed second grade, and by his records at Taft, he did quite well—didn't he?" questioned Mary Jane Andrews.

"Well, yes he has, but he does have some skill weaknesses in second grade that the Taft teachers didn't catch."

"Are you telling me that Jared really did not complete second grade at Taft, that he didn't or shouldn't have passed?" questioned Mrs. Andrews with a firmness she could not believe she managed.

"No, not exactly that," said Miss Johnson.

"Well, then, are you telling me that Mrs. Wahlstom at Taft was not a competent teacher, that she didn't know that Jared had problems or, as you said, skill weaknesses?"

"I'm not saying that either," exclaimed Miss Johnson. "These skill deficiencies are not always easy to detect, and I'm sure that Mrs. Wahlstom knew of their existence and was probably working on them."

"What skill deficiencies does Jared have?" asked Mrs. Andrews for the tenth time in the last three months.

"That's part of our problem, we're not sure we know the whole answer. And even then the business of just where Jared is to be placed is kind of open. But to answer your question, we've tested Jared three or four times and have been drilling him on about eight skills that the tests showed to be real weaknesses. As far as instruction is concerned, we've just put him in second grade materials because we feel he can handle most of that material. It will give us more time to locate his problems more definitively."

"The whole thing sounds like a big guessing game to me," said Mrs. Andrews. "It sounds very unsophisticated; kind of like a game of roulette!"

"I can assure you that that is not the case, Mrs. Andrews, but you must understand that meeting the needs of twenty-five children is no easy task," retorted Miss Johnson.

"I'm sure it isn't, but I'm only concerned about my child. What happens if you don't find his correct place and he doesn't start to learn?" queried Mrs. Andrews.

"Oh, you won't have to worry about that," said Miss Johnson, "we'll find out where he belongs, and he'll be just fine."

"Is that a guarantee?"

"Of course, I can't make such a guarantee. But you can rest assured we'll do our best," smiled Miss Johnson.

"Unfortunately I'm not overwhelmed with confidence," commented Mrs. Andrews with no small degree of sarcasm in her voice.

"I'm sorry you feel that way," said Miss Johnson, "we will do our best."

"Well, I guess that will have to do for the time being, but Todd and I are convinced we will not let things continue like this for another year. We'll try to have a specialist see Jared and if necessary get him into another school next year."

"Whatever you think is best, Mrs. Andrews, the school will cooperate in every way possible," assured Miss Johnson. "Thank you for coming in."

Mrs. Andrews left the conference room at Robins Elementary with a feeling of complete frustration.

As Miss Johnson was gathering her conference papers together to leave the school for the day, Miss Adams, the fifth grade teacher greeted her, "Hi, Sylvia, how was the conference?"

Sylvia Johnson frowned.

The preceding story though not an actual case study accurately depicts any of hundreds of daily parent and teacher exchanges in school systems in the United States. It portrays the tenor, content, and frustration of parents and teachers engaged in what must appear to be a very unsophisticated process for warding off student failure and increasing student learning. It illustrates several basic flaws in school system program design that cloud the instructional future for many students and casts serious doubts on whether or not school systems will be able to direct meaningful forces on the resolution of student failure.

The story is not posed to deprecate the intent of career educators or to impeach the efforts of school systems or their personnel. Rather, it is presented to illustrate the exceedingly delicate position in which thousands and thousands of conscientious teachers and administrators find themselves when trying to respond to why students like Jared Andrews are failing in our school systems. Unquestionably, no one would have been happier than Miss Johnson to have been able to identify specifically the causes of Jared's recent failures and detail an educational roadmap on how those failures would be overcome shortly. If she could not have provided that detailed roadmap to success for Jared, Miss Johnson, like many educators, would have been relieved to admit that sometimes the educational process does include a great deal of "guessing," is "unsophisticated," and may be "likened to a game of roulette." She would have been forthright in saying that school systems often do not have sophisticated tools for effectively locating learning problems and quickly remedying them. Many times the absence of these tools reduces the teaching-learning process for under-achieving, disadvantaged, disabled, and reluctant learners to a gigantic "shell game" where learning problems are hidden or unknown and easily elude the valiant, but futile, attempts of educators to guess their location. Reluctantly, such conditions force many administrators and teachers to give up on students. Unable to find the location and substance of the complex combination of learning deficiencies, they simply admit failure. In the case of Jared Andrews, neither the teacher nor the Andrews were about to admit failure, but the signs of impending failure were clear—erratic testing, placement, and instruction and mounting teacher, parent, and student frustration.

The critical determinant in whether or not Jared Andrews and most other students will succeed or fail in school is the teacher. If teachers locate the sources of learning problems and take appropriate corrective and preventative actions, a student will most likely respond and learn. If the learning problems are not located and corrected, the student will begin a succession of failures that will terminate when his school experience terminates. Certainly, there is the probability that other teachers may locate the student's problems, but the probability of this occurring declines rapidly as the student continues in school and his instruction becomes further and further removed from the origin of his learning problems. Succeeding teachers usually see factors related to the original problems and rarely have the means or the time to trace the problems to their roots. This is particularly true of the teacher whose task it is to eliminate two or three year old learning problems. In most instances, they fail at resolving the learning problems and stemming student failure.

School System Instructional Vulnerability

The conference between Mary Jane Andrews and Sylvia Johnson serves to dramatize the prevailing vulnerability of most school system instructional programs in the United States. Rather than inspiring the concerned parent, it questions the ability of school systems to accommodate instructionally all children. Further, it causes dedicated and professionally competent educators to appear disorganized, illprepared, and unknowledgeable about the interworkings of the instructional programs they dispense.

It poses the possibility that major flaws exist in the processes educators employ to locate the symptoms of student failure and to eradicate them. It suggests that many students will begin failing at a very early point in the schooling process, and though the signs of failure will be recognized by both the teacher and parent, the tools vital to the location and correction of learning problems will be neither sophisticated enough nor sufficiently detailed enough to help the teacher or student reverse failure.

It is unlikely that either Mary Jane Andrews or Sylvia Johnson recognized the significance of Mrs. Andrews's incisive inquiries, but with a few perfectly directed questions, she managed to strike the most vulnerable nerves of the school systems' instructional programs. She established that Robins Elementary School, Taft Elementary School, and presumably the remainder of the schools in the system in which her child was enrolled, lacked program continuity. Apparently the system had not identified its instructional skills, concepts, and processes for programs offered. It had made no effort to coordinate textual series from one school to the next in the same program areas. Thus, the school system was illprepared to facilitate the smooth movement of some students from one school to another. She ascertained that the system had little confidence in its standardized achievement testing program and that the back-up testing systems, the diagnostic tests, provided information that was erratic, inconclusive, and possibly exceedingly inaccurate. She learned that instructional placement cannot be accomplished successfully without an accurate determination of skill weaknesses and that the skill weaknesses could not be ascertained without effective diagnostic tests. She heard that tentative placement is often a procedure implemented to give the educator time to reinvestigate an uncertain and confusing set of circumstances. She recognized that tentative placement is often accompanied by instructing the student at a textual level that may already have been mastered. She was aware that this combination of circumstances spells impending failure.

Had Mary Jane Andrews recognized the significance of her own questions and the implications of Miss Johnson's responses, she could have ruptured the aura of public education in America. She would have learned that often school systems are most vulnerable in their proclaimed bastion: the instructional programs.

Indeed, school systems are exceedingly vulnerable to public criticism. They do not have the capacity to fulfill the expectation that each student will be accorded indefective assistance that will ensure maximal learning for the average, the gifted, the retarded, the disadvantaged, and the learning disabled child. School systems simply are not confident about the effectiveness of the processes and the tools they employ to detect student strengths and weaknesses, nor are they certain about the tactics and devices that hold promise for alleviating identified problems. Too often testing systems, if they exist at all, are flawed; skill content has not been specified to a degree that the teacher has the guidance and confidence to know the desired results of programs; instructional materials are often incomplete or inadequate for treating students with learning problems; school organization may militate against flexibility in grouping students or carrying out individualized instruction for students requiring specialized instruction; staff arrangements may prohibit the sharing of ideas and the pooling of resources; or the school system's direction and philosophy may inadvertently prohibit the conduct of instructional programs in a manner best suited to the needs of students with learning problems (as in the case where a textual selection requires whole group instruction or a school schedule prohibits cross-grade grouping or an open-campus plan reduces teacher access to failing students).

Most school administrators and teachers partially recognize the vulnerability of school system instructional programs. They are pointed out directly by educational critics and, inadvertently, they are illustrated almost daily in encounters with parents or students. It is a rare administrator or teacher who does not want to attack the problematic areas of instructional programming and correct the flaws that prove to be unexplainable to parents and embarrassing to all educators. The teacher would like to envision the conference where she could meet the parents of her poorest student and relate to them with confidence: "I have tested your child and determined that he should be placed instructionally at *this* point in our textual materials. His diagnostic results illustrate weaknesses in *these* specific skills. My colleagues and I are reinforcing *these* skills on a supplemental basis with *these* materials. Since placing your child in appropriate materials and providing basic and supplemental instruction, he has progressed to *this* point—which demonstrates excellent progress. As his teacher, I'd like you to assist us in working on the reinforcement of *these* skills at home. Here are materials and activities you can use to that end. Do you have any questions?"

Can educators ever hope to have this type of self-assured dialogue with parents? Most certainly they can. It does require, however, that school systems and individual teachers undertake a reexamination of the design and organization of their instructional programs. This does not suggest that their programs should be or will be discarded, but rather, that they need to be specified more clearly and exactly so that it is possible to tell why certain things happen to some students and what can be done about the failures that students encounter.

This book is not a panacea for all of the ills of school system instructional programs. Nevertheless, it suggests that the more knowledgeable educators are about their programs, the more exacting they are in diagnosing students, the more effective they are in affixing a student's placement for instruction, and the more flexible they are in acquiring the most effective learning materials, the more likely educators are to be accurate in making judgments about students in the learning process. In addition, it suggests that the more educators know about the content of their instructional programs, the more likely it is that the temporary failures of students will be a valuable part of the educators' learning process. Thus, on the next occasion where similar learning problems arise, the teacher will be far better prepared to deal with it from a knowledgeable base of past experience.

The content of this book focuses on four points of instructional program vulnerability: the instructional program foundation (the skills, processes, concepts, and elements upon which any program of instruction is based); diagnosis; placement; and prescription (instruction as a result of diagnosis). Each of those facets of programming is examined by providing a general definition of the process, the values of that process, design work that can be undertaken on a school system basis to improve the process, design work that can be undertaken by the teacher to use the process (generally in the event that the system fails to undertake design activities), and examples and illustrations of documents that may be developed to use with each of the processes.

It is hoped that the reader will conclude the book with a broader understanding of the importance of each of the four instructional processes and a procedure for reorganizing instructional programs and their delivery. In the final analysis, such a critical look at instructional program design may assist larger numbers of administrators and teachers to find greater degrees of satisfaction in solving the complex problems that prevent many students from achieving their individual capabilities.

2.   The Instructional
Program Foundation

All instructional programs in school systems are created to convey skills to students. The various combination of skills (also called concepts and processes) are the building blocks for every program or course of study, and the purposes of programs are to insure that students will master, experience, or be exposed to the critical, identified skills. The skills, concepts, and processes of a program or course, are so important that were they not identified, the school system and its teachers would have no formal direction for teaching. In addition, it would be most difficult to carry out accurate student diagnosis, placement, program assessment, or pupil assessment. Herein lies a problem. Many school districts and most state departments of education have failed to give leadership to teachers by identifying the specific skills, concepts, and processes that are critical for instruction. The teacher is basically on his or her own to carry out a program successfully and accountably with little or no guidance beyond a textbook.

Instructional Program Foundation Defined

An instructional program foundation is the combination of skills, concepts, and processes that constitutes a program or course of study. Every subject (kindergarten reading readiness, home economics, advanced calculus) contains a set of skills, concepts, or processes that the school system will convey to the student and later assess to determine mastery, experience, or exposure. That set of skills for kindergarten reading readiness is the subject's instructional program foundation.

Instructional program foundations for programs or courses of study are virtually always focused on one or any combination of three goals: developing basic literacy; developing or instilling conventions or customs; and developing readiness or facility for immediate or future employment.

Basic literacy skills include such understandable elements as reading; mathematical concepts; handwriting and spelling processes; rudimentary music and art skills; historical concepts and perspectives of a factual nature; and a range of others. The skills of convention and custom vary from prescribed ones (laws, rules, procedures) to more implied permissive ones (attitudes, values, morals, ethics). Employment skills are varied depending upon the course offerings of a school system and are open to individual choice (selection of a course of study or a future career) except where the individual student's abilities limit his employment options.

Regardless of the course of study pursued by a student, the school system and its teachers will be delivering instructional content to the student in the form of skills, concepts, and processes that are focused on basic literacy, conventions and customs, and immediate or future employment. It is crucial that a school system and its teachers be fully aware of the instructional foundations they are delivering, the focus of the instructional foundation (literacy, convention, custom, employment), whether or not the student is acquiring them, the degree to which acquisition is taking place, and what should be done in the event that such learning is not taking place. These were among the obvious failings of the Robins Elementary instructional program when Sylvia Johnson attempted to explain something that had neither logic nor direction.

The Values of an Instructional Program Foundation

Foundations for school system instructional programs provide a wealth of information about the plan for instruction in a local community. Using listings of skills, concepts, and processes, teachers and parents are able to review the direction of programs; their skill content; the criteria that will be used in diagnosing and placing students; the scope of instruction and prescription; and the basis for assessing programs, procedures, and students. Most important, the instructional program foundation furnishes educators and parents with a common base for communicating about a student's progress or about the program in which he or she is enrolled.

Direction of Programs. Every type of organization and every program operated by an organization require specific directions for it to accomplish some worthwhile ends. Just as a Sunday School nursery program and a complex corporation specify and carry out stated skills and tasks to accomplish larger goals and objectives, school system instructional programs need the documentation of skills that specify all of the steps that will take a student from a point of little or no knowledge to one of advanced knowledge (for example, from a non-reader to a proficient reader; a selfish, self-centered child to a socially-responsive young adult; an enthusiastic novice to a basically proficient draftsman). One function of the instructional program foundation is to specify the plan of action—including each elemental skill—that a school system is employing to assist the student in reaching a specific set of objectives or outcomes in each course and program. At the conclusion of a course of study or program, all students will not necessarily have achieved the objectives or outcomes, but some progress should have been made. The instructional program foundation, in this instance, serves as a gauge for helping the teacher and parent determine whether or not the program and student are on target.

School systems that have not specified their instructional program foundations lack direction. This does not necessarily mean that the students enrolled in the school system will not learn to read, compute mathematics, or converse in French, but it does increase the probability that (1) programs and courses of the same titles offered in the school system (Chemistry 1 and Chemistry 1) will not emphasize the same skills, concepts, and processes; (2) students who have problems in a course or program will have an increased possibility of failing because diagnosis of their problems will be faulty when skills are not known or understood; (3) more frequently will students be incorrectly placed for instruction; (4) programs conducted in sequence (English 7 and English 8) will have little continuity and exaggerate problems of articulation for students with learning problems; (5) assessments and comparisons of identical programs and courses will have no meaning; and (6) little individualized instruction can be attempted on a concerted basis.

The direction of instructional programs is vitally important if there is to be any hope that students will receive an equal opportunity to succeed. Programs without direction confuse teachers and students and often cause them to fail at their tasks. For the teacher failure can be overcome with future successes, but for the failing student the possibility of future success is greatly diminished.

Diagnosis. The well constructed instructional program foundation serves educators as a tool for student diagnosis. When the basic skills, concepts, and processes of a program or course are identified and defined, local tests can be constructed and administered to determine students' learning strengths and weaknesses. Such tests direct the teacher's attention to program skills that have persistently caused student failure in the past and pinpoint those which are important enough not to be left unattended lest they compound and prolong failure in the future. Additionally, diagnosis frequently identifies spots in programs where skills are poorly sequenced, coordinated, or articulated. It also illustrates instances where instruction was erratic, too rapid, confusing, or poorly represented by textual materials—all matters that can be corrected if instructional program foundations are completely specified and available for careful teacher and school system scrutiny.

Those school systems that have not developed instructional program foundations rarely have meaningful diagnostic test devices available for the teachers. Rather, because skills, concepts, and processes are not identified and cannot be used to construct internal instruments with closer correlation to local programs, they are forced to rely on test instruments unrelated to their system's programs. The data they gather and apply have marginal utility and value for making decisions about student learning problems and school system instructional programs. In many instances, the application of external diagnostic and achievement test data to programs without foundations is mere guesswork and causes as many problems as it solves. It is conceivable that intuitive reasoning about a child's instructional problems may be more accurate than the data gathered from test instruments that have a questionable relationship to the school's program. But in the absence of an instructional program foundation, the teacher's judgment may be the more effective diagnostic tool.

Placement. Just as the instructional program foundation serves as a basis for diagnosing students, it can also be used for the determination of student placement positions in programs. The more elaborate and refined the instructional program foundation and the diagnostic tests derived from it are, the more exact will be the student's placement.

Accurate placement in an instructional program vastly increases the likelihood that students will learn because they will receive instruction commensurate with previously acquired skills. They will not be expected to relearn skills previously mastered nor begin instruction in content for which they are illprepared. An accurate assessment of student placement accounts for each skill in which mastery has been demonstrated, builds upon them, and attacks and strengthens those in which students have exhibited weakness.

The school system that has not developed instructional program foundations is in a severely disadvantaged position to place students. Not knowing what skills are essential to the mastery of a program or the sequence in which the skills are most logically introduced reduces diagnostic accuracy. That, in turn, confounds the accuracy of placement for nearly all but those students who are on grade level or very near to it. The greater the diagnostic and placement errors are, the greater is the probability that the student will fail, especially if placement is inaccurate by a half grade level or more.

Unfortunately, teachers' guessing about student placement is far less accurate than their guessing about skill weaknesses. A teacher may be able to use tests that are unrelated to a school system's program or administer self-devised inventories and still determine student deficiencies with some degree of accuracy, but determining where the student should be placed in the formal textual and supplemental materials is an entirely different matter. Because of the repetitive nature of many programs, a skill may be introduced and retaught at higher levels of sophistication nearly a dozen times at several grade levels and in a multitude of contexts. Correctly guessing at which precise point the student should be placed under these circumstances is highly improbable, and thus the student will often receive inappropriate instruction.

Instruction/Prescription. It is around the skills, processes, and concepts of programs and courses that instructional units are developed and classroom teaching is organized. Instructional units are the written plans for delivering skills to a wide variety of students of varied ability. Knowledge of an instructional program foundation's skills, concepts, and processes enables the classroom teacher to accumulate or develop a variety of instructional materials and media that can be drawn upon to teach from in a multitude of different contents and with a variety of methodologies. Such variations in presentation increase the likelihood that students with different styles of learning will acquire skills upon initial exposure—presuming that the student has been correctly diagnosed and placed for instruction.

The absence of instructional program foundations handicaps teachers in the design of instructional units and in preplanning for student needs. Material and media selection and sequencing becomes time consuming, inaccurate, and sometimes impossible. A classroom teacher may recognize that students have problems when they enter a program or during the course of the program, but an inability to pinpoint important foundation skills prohibits the early location of materials that will be most appropriate to remedy them as they become evident later on in the program. In similar instances, newly marketed textbooks or supplemental materials that have been determined to be promising are difficult to integrate with an undefined instructional program foundation and existing, poorly detailed materials. This prevents or at least restricts teachers from the controlled substitution of potentially sound instructional units because of the fear that they may meet with less success than standard materials being employed. The insecurity that reinforces the use of only moderately successful instructional units in the place of highly promising ones is an example of how the absence of instructional program foundations fosters program stagnation. The result is program content that remains virtually unchanged over a period of years, even though substantial numbers of students have been unsuccessful in programs.

Teaching students with learning problems involves a certain degree of educated risk taking if there are to be hopes that these students will make significant learning gains. However, in the absence of instructional program foundations, the risks may be too great for teachers to assume. Certainly the teachers who have tried and failed to develop and convey creative instructional units that would help all students learn are less likely to be so venturesome when problems next present themselves. That is particularly true if the school administrator and parents misinterpreted the teachers' efforts and complain. Moreover, school systems that are slow to identify and to define their instructional program foundations will more often than not culture cautious and conservative teachers who will avoid striking program innovation—sometimes to the detriment of those students who need programs with special tailoring.

Program Assessment. The skill information furnished by instructional program foundations enables school administrators and teachers to assess the effectiveness of programs and courses. In a manner similar to developing tests to diagnose student learning strengths and weaknesses, test instruments can be constructed to determine the degree to which students have acquired skills, concepts, and processes. These tests indicate the degree to which programs and courses have been successful in achieving their goals and objectives. They will also illustrate a program's strengths, weaknesses, and repetitions and expose the degree to which these characteristics prevail throughout a school or a system. Such information is important for suggesting means for program improvement through curriculum development or refinement, inservice education, realignment of school system spending priorities, revision of instructional groups, staffing changes, or other controlled program manipulations.

School systems without instructional program foundations are in a disadvantaged position when conducting program assessment because they are without the means to assess program success, failure, strengths, or weaknesses. Under these conditions, somewhat arbitrary assessment instruments are usually acquired or devised to measure the unstated skills, concepts, and processes in the program. As one might suspect, such a procedure usually provides an assessment of highly questionable accuracy with little concrete relationship to the skills and the content provided to students in the classroom. It poses great possibilities for offending and harming staff members because, more often than not, the measurement criteria would not have been known by teachers before the program was initiated, and thus no opportunities would have arisen to align the program with the assessment instrument. Data provided by such ex post facto testing are of little value to administrators, teachers, or programs. They may reflect strengths and weaknesses exhibited by students on the test, but these features may not be a "commonly held" part of the unidentified instructional program foundation or textual content used in the classroom. In an equal number of instances, the program assessment may omit a substantial number of skills commonly believed to be central to the program, or it may identify nothing more than the wide differences that characterize teachers' beliefs on what is or is not the skill content of a program.

Inaccuracy is the one characteristic that will typify assessments in school systems without instructional program foundations. Programs, courses, and grade levels that do not have skills identified and defined cannot be assessed validly, and any inferences drawn from their assessment may be subject to severe criticism. Certainly, it is very unlikely that much program improvement will be fostered by this type of assessment.

Base for Communication. The presence of instructional program foundations in written form in a school system provides a base for communications between educators and the public concerning the direction and content of local programs. Instructional program foundations remove much of the mystique surrounding the content of programs and encourage the exchange of information about students and the most effective means of instructing them. It affords parents an opportunity to become more knowledgeable about, involved in, and sympathetic toward an institution in which they have their tax dollars invested and from which they expect a substantial return through the education of their children. The commitment of community patrons to local programs fostered through their exposure to program foundations can return substantial dividends to the school system. Citizens who feel they have an understanding of instructional skills, concepts, and processes and who recognize the complexity of providing quality instruction to students are far more sympathetic to increased teacher salaries, program changes, facility improvement, and the expansion of supportive services than are local patrons who have been excluded from affecting program and policy decisions about their schools. Even local boards of education are often denied access to instructional program foundations and thus cannot speak favorably or knowledgeably about the worth of programs. In this light, it is little wonder that boards of education demonstrate some skepticism about or outright opposition to program innovations or expansions that require additional tax dollars.

Perhaps the greatest advantage of opening up instructional program foundations to the public for examination is in availing the opportunity for participatory program development. To some degree, programs should reflect the skills, processes, and concepts that the community perceives to be important. Sometimes educators are presumptuous about skills that "should" be added to programs and guarded about "who will do the adding." Although educators are often better qualified than noneducators to refine or to revise programs it should not lead to the exclusion of the public whose children are the recipients of program content from being involved in program specification. Most parents are not concerned about being excluded from the development of instructional programs in a school system, but they should still reserve the right to examine program foundations and voice their opinions about their directions, clarity, priorities, and effectiveness. The presence of instructional program foundations ensures parents that that option is preserved and strengthened and there will exist a sound base for communication between educators and their communities.

Designing the Instructional Program Foundation

Building instructional program foundations for school system programs is not unlike the construction of any other tangible product. A definite end product must be in mind before creation begins, and fairly specific plans of action must precede developmental work. Educators will want to consider skill identification, classes of skills, the mix of skills, skill relationships, skill revisions, skill transportability, and examples and parallels in other programs outside the school system.

Skill Identification. Prior to beginning skill, concept, and process identification, educators must determine, in at least a general way, what is to be accomplished by conducting a course or a program. Some generally stated course or program objectives will help to set a tone for determining the skills that will be subsequently identified. As an example, the following general result may be stated for kindergarten reading:

> It is important that our students be ready to handle a preprimer within a week or so after they enter first grade.

Now, this statement is far from a complex behavioral objective and it is not *perfectly* clear, but it causes educators to focus on one or more points of reference (in this case a preprimer) before beginning skill, concept, and process identification. In this instance it has fulfilled its purpose. The teachers examining the reading program can review the school system's and other preprimers and logically ask: "To what do we have to introduce children in kindergarten to make it plausible that they will be able to function in this preprimer by September of next year." Teachers can then conceive a range of skills that may include visual discrimination of colors, shapes, and letters, auditory discrimination of sounds, letters of the alphabet, and so on.

The same general procedure can be established for any course or program in the school system's curricula. In a junior high school general music course, for example, educators may generally concede that they would like a course with the following general results:

> Our students should learn about past and contemporary musical authors; a range of musical instruments; musical terminology and format. . . .

Out of this statement, questions such as "which ones, how much, when, to what degree, how well," are the important steps that lead to skill investigation and identification. Eventually, statements about courses and programs become refined to the point that they look and sound more like the following program result for auto mechanics:

> On a written test and in laboratory activities the student will perform fifteen specified job entry level skills commonly expected of apprentice auto mechanics as identified by the school system's technical advisory committee. The skills will be demonstrated during a three hour time block and must be rated at or above average performance by the rating team.

Even though the phrasing of this statement is more precise and perhaps looks more academic, it is important to note that teachers will still need to ask the penetrating questions: which skills? how much? when? to what degree? how well? and so forth. When these questions are addressed, skill, concept, and process identification is underway.

Skill identification for a program or course is not carried out in isolation and is rarely undertaken anew. It is usually undertaken using a backlog of information already accumulated. After reviewing the objectives or results of a program, any or all of the following procedures may be used to ascertain those skills that will maximize student learning and program goal attainment:

- Examine the content of materials adopted by the school system and used in its programs. (Examination of the reading series used in the school system, for example, would be appropriate to being locating reading skills essential to the accomplishment of reading program objectives).
- Apply the knowledge acquired by expert teachers who have taught or are trained to teach the program.
- Examine the content and logic of a range of authors and texts dealing with the program.
- Examine the content and priorities of reputable diagnostic tests available for that program.
- Review other pertinent literature on the program.
- Review research studies on the program.
- Identify the skills in tentative form.
- Subject the skills to a review by internal subject matter consultants, external consultants, or university staff members.
- Subject the skills to a review by teams of school system teachers, administrators (usually principals or subject matter supervisors), and parents.
- Complete the skills for dissemination and usage.
- Set plans for annually reviewing and assessing the skills.

After skills are identified, it is important to determine the sequence of the program and set priorities on those skills that are most crucial. Such a determination will prevent the inexperienced or the unwary from underrating the impact that omitting or slighting prominent skills may have on students already exhibiting skill weaknesses. Validation of the skill sequence and priorities of a program will most likely take the same form as the original validation of program skills.

Educators will need to remember that there is great latitude in identifying skills, concepts, and processes for school system programs. In effect, the skill content of instructional programs can encompass "anything that educators state and the community affirms is valuable for the instruction of students in the school system." Traditionally, of course, there are many skills that are commonly accepted by educators and community patrons as central to "all school system curricula." These skills are generally the basic literacy skills, some of the skills of custom and convention, and basic employment skills for programs offered or promoted in the school system. These skills are standard fare in programs and should be maintained. At the same time there are hundreds of skills presented in commercial instructional materials that may or may not be basic to or desirable for local instructional programs. Such skills, however, may be added to or deleted from the school system's final instructional foundation in order to attain the local objectives. Likewise, there are skills, concepts, and processes not presented in commercial materials that may be thought important to reflect local flavor, traditions, interests, or values (the *Fox Fire* books, for example).

Generally, educators, almost at the total exclusion of the public, will play the predominant role in investigating and identifying the skill content of local programs. This, in part, will be due to the skepticism, disinterest, philosophical fragmentation and perceived unsophistication of local citizens. Such a potential vacuum in program development necessitates increased caution by educators, who are tempted to affix total instructional skill content without any community validation, even from the local board of education. This type of instructional foundation design is the very stuff that may erode the confidence that communities presumably would like to have in "their" schools. School system administrators and teachers will do well to challenge their community patrons to review and react to program and course foundations both to determine that programs are on target and, more importantly, to illustrate their intent to be forthright and open about directions, priorities, and content that will be delivered to students.

Classes of Skills. As teachers are examining the skills, concepts, and processes they have identified, they will want to be mindful of the tendency in most school systems to overemphasize the factual learning skills in programs almost at the exclusion of all other types of skills. There are three classes of skills that make up school system instructional programs: those treating factual information (cognitive skills); value, moral, ethical, and attitudinal issues (affective skills); and motor facility (psychomotor skills). It is important that all three classes of skills be represented in instructional programs where such representation is appropriate.

An important question about what is being taught in schools today is whether or not students value the factual content they are learning enough to ever use it. Thus, ignoring affective and psychomotor skills in instructional program design can be a serious error because without them questions of attitude and value will never be assessed and, therefore, determinations of program success will remain incomplete. For example, a reading program may be assessed both on the basis of acquired factual skills as well as whether or not students enjoy, value, or have positive attitudes about the program (affective). The same point applies equally well to a wide range of other programs or courses. In social studies, for example, it may be as important to assess a student's attitudes (affective) about the Emancipation Proclamation as his knowledge of what it is, when and why it happened; and under what conditions it was written (cognitive). Likewise, it is more valuable to assess a student's actual ability to steer a car (psychomotor), make a mitre cut (psychomotor), repair a metal lathe (psychomotor), or type a business letter (psychomotor) than to describe, list, or respond to questions (cognitive) about such activities.

Such skills, concepts, and processes become integrated into instructional programs and courses because they are identified by teachers as being important. Consequently, teachers must consider the focuses of programs beyond mere factual skill delivery and ask whether or not select value and motor skills ought to be included in program content, taught, assessed, and used as criteria for determining total program or course success.

Mix of Skills. Finding the right combination or "mix" of cognitive, affective, or psychomotor skills that make up a program or course is not easy. There is no quota system, no formula, no shortcut that would have general applicability to all school systems. Nonetheless, teachers will need to devote some time to considering what would seem like a fair balance for their programs and courses as skills, concepts, and processes are identified.

Most school systems will want some cognitive, affective, and psychomotor skills taught in all courses. Too often, however, there is no guidance about just how much "some" is. If the school system has developed guiding objectives, they will provide some indication of the emphasis of a skill mix. In other instances, philosophy statements provide some, but not much, guidance.

Where no information is available, experimentation will be required, but it will need to be undertaken with a large measure of common sense. There can be the possibility of serious program distortion if the mix of skills is dramatically varied from a normal pattern of school system operation. As an example, there have been occasions where—in the name of value education—reading programs have been altered to a point where the students are free to make all choices in reading materials and move freely about the classroom discussing reading activities with other students and the teacher in the place of formal instruction. Two results of one such program were that students thoroughly enjoyed the reading class and, in fact, even read a greater number of books than previously. Two other results were that the students consistently selected "easy" materials that were enjoyable, though not mentally taxing, and their actual reading levels failed to improve. The results of the program may or may not present a problem, depending upon the stated objectives of the program. However, if the mix of skills did not reflect the intent of the program, it will need to be adjusted to insure that students are receiving a balance that is desired by the school system and, ultimately, most valuable to the student in the long run.

Perhaps the soundest test of a program or course skill mix can be obtained by submitting the skills, concepts, and processes to principals and other teachers and asking for a truthful assessment of how well the balance seems. Teachers who consider themselves somewhat "conservative" may do well to ask for at least one assessment from a teacher they think has a "liberal" (if not "radical") curriculum philosophy.

Relationships Among Skills. Identifying skills, concepts, and processes requires some awareness of the relationships of skills in instructional programs. Skill relationships are little more than the patterns or sequences in which skills are arranged in instructional materials to add to the logic of a program, aid the student in making transitions from skill to skill or lesson to lesson, and increase the probability of greater student learning. Teachers will want to be knowledgeable about skill relationships to assist them in identifying, sequencing, diagnosing, instructing, and assessing skills, concepts, and processes and selecting materials.

A few skill relationships that are commonly found in commercially prepared materials are the hierarchical, cyclical, unitized, and random relationships. Many of these relationships are frequently found interwoven or hybridized in instructional materials.

Hierarchical skill relationships are arrangements of skills in a form similar to a step ladder or pyramid. Mastery of one skill or combination of skills is a prerequisite for mastery of successive skills. Thus, hierarchical skill relationships are organized in a sequence that presents the simplist skill first and graduates to more and more difficult skills. The mastery of a difficult skill is based on the mastery of the simpler skills. This type of skill relationship could be conceptualized as:

> Skill 1
> Skill 2
> Skill 3
> Skill 4
> ... and so forth.

Cyclical skill relationships are arrangements of skills that incorporate (1) the introduction of skills in a successively more difficult, but related, sequence (hierarchical) and (2) frequently repeating or reviewing skills introduced earlier to the student. The cyclical skill relationship can best be visualized as a loop, and follows a sequence that may be stated as follows: easy skill, more difficult skill, most difficult skill, repeat easy skill.... The earlier hierarchical skill relationship tended to rely on student learning through information transfer (the application of something simple and known to learn something more difficult and unknown). Cyclical skill relationships also employ that feature but add to it the notion of repetition or reinforcement. This type of skill relationship may be conceptualized as:

> Skill 1
> Skill 2
> Skill 3
> Skill 4
> Skill 2
> Skill 3
> Skill 4
> Skill 5
> Skill 6
> ... and so forth.

Unitized skill relationships are arrangements of skills in blocks or units. A block contains a series of skills, concepts, or processes that are directed at a specific theme, and the skills within the block are often sequenced hierarchically or cyclically. Normally, one block of skills may have little or no relationship to a previous or subsequent block of skills. As such, a block may be viewed as a somewhat self-contained unit and often can be rearranged from one section of a program to another without confusion to the student or a loss of program continuity. This cannot be accomplished with programs that are hierarchically or cyclically constructed.

Unitized skill relationships are frequently found in higher level instructional programs (English programs, social studies programs, science programs, an array of career-technical programs, and others). This type of skill relationship could be conceptualized as:

Skill 1
Skill 2
Skill 3
Skill 4

Skill 12
Skill 13
Skill 14
Skill 15
. . . and so forth.

Random skill relationships are skill arrangements that seemingly have little consistent form or pattern. Occasionally, this occurs because programs are poorly constructed; on other occasions, the skills are just not naturally related, and, hence, there is minimal relationship between one set and other sets of skills. In either instance, the skill relationships change so frequently that a certain amount of deductive logic is required to establish the relationship between sets of skills. Random skill relationships, like unitized ones, need not necessarily be taught at an established point in a program, but they will need to be treated somewhere. These skill relationships are frequently found in higher level instructional programs that cannot be easily unitized or where unitizing does not measurably increase the logic of the program (for example, medical diagnosis, automotive diagnosis, physics, and others). This type of skill relationship could be conceptualized as:

Skill 1
Skill 2
Skill 23
Skill 8
Skill 2
Skill 18
... and so forth.

All four of the skill relationships examined above—and hybrid combinations of them—are found in textbooks and school system programs. Hierarchical and cyclical skill relationships tend to occur more frequently though not exclusively in elementary school programs that are oriented toward basic literacy instruction. Unitized and random skill relationships tend to predominate in elementary and secondary programs emphasizing conventions and customs and secondary programs oriented toward employment. Hierarchical and cyclical programs tend toward a heavy cognitive emphasis. Unitized and random skill programs may emphasize any or all of the skill classes.

As educators design instructional program foundations, it would be beneficial to examine the types of skill relationships that hold the most promise for improving student learning. Though there may not often be information available to indicate a "best way" to organize an instructional foundation, skill relationships that build on learning transfer (hierarchical) and a degree of review or reenforcement (cyclical) leave skill acquisition less to chance and insight than do unitized and random patterns and, therefore, increase the probability that more students will acquire skills on initial exposure. At the same time, student diagnosis and placement is much more easily accomplished when hierarchical and cyclical skill patterns are used than when unitized and random skill sequences are used.

Skill Revisions. Most school system program skills tend to change rather infrequently. Though the content materials used to present skills change very rapidly (as witnessed by improvements in textual, workbook, and audio-visual materials), the skills, concepts, and processes weather frequent philosophical and methodological storms and remain relatively constant. This is particularly true of programs whose focal thrust is toward basic literacy skills. For example, there has not been dramatic change in the basic skills of reading, English usage, spelling, handwriting, and mathematics at the elementary school level in years, even though the content and context that have been used to convey skills to students have changed considerably. By the same token, skills of convention and custom have changed considerably with the passage of time, but large blocks of skills have remained totally unchanged (particularly historical records of events, basic governmental tenets, laws, and human relations).

Employment skills have undergone the greatest modification with the passage of time and promise to continue to change far more rapidly in the future. Changes in technology have rendered many jobs obsolete, and past training for these jobs is either inappropriate or has undergone sweeping change. Consequently, instructional programs designed to convey employment skills need to be updated frequently.

Revising instructional program skills—as identifying them originally—involves a validation of those that may be added to, retained in, or dropped from instructional programs. Employment skills will need to be correlated with present and projected trends on the regional labor market and validated by individuals who are functioning in the labor market. Skills of convention and custom can be validated through observation of and communication with local community patrons and the broader society. Literacy skills can, in the main, be referenced to past and present practices and tempered with the scanty research that is available on sound curriculum revision.

Transporting Skills. Normally, educators working on identifying skills, concepts, and processes would give little thought to whether or not such activities have any relationship to the use of instructional materials developed in other school systems. It is a thought that merits a good deal of consideration, however. Nearly every school district engages in some form of curriculum design, and those that have meticulously developed their program foundation can integrate quality materials from other districts to their own as enhancements to the material resources available to their students. Transporting skills and materials from one school system to another and integrating them into a local curricula is a low cost way of expanding already superb program options for students. School systems that have developed program foundations can take advantage of the transportability feature of many program skills; districts with no defined program foundations cannot.

Skills, concepts, processes, and the materials used to instruct them in most school system programs can be transported from one locality to another with little modification. Though most school systems believe their instructional programs are unique, large blocks of skill content in programs are much the same from district to district. Indeed, one does find wide variance in the textual materials, styles, and methodologies used to teach program skills in school systems, and the sequence of skills does vary from one commercial program to the next. But in a cross-sampling of skills in several district algebra, earth science, general music, drafting, American history, and third grade reading programs (to mention only a few) all of which employed different texts and philosophies, it was found that there was less than 10 percent variance in the program skills among all of the school systems. The reason for the low variance is that school systems undertake little original skill, concept, and process identification themselves but, rather, accept the skills contained in commercially prepared materials without much modification after they are purchased. At the same time, commercial firms generally produce a product that incorporates a relatively standard set of skills cloaked in new terminology, better print, more detailed referencing, more colorful illustrations, and unlimited gadgetry.

Some generalizations can be made about skill transportability. Programs with a cognitive skill emphasis can be transported from system to system with less modification than can affective or psychomotor programs. Basic literacy and employment faculty skills can be transported more easily than skills of convention and custom. Elementary school program skills can be transported with less adjustment than secondary program skills, though most secondary programs can be easily transported.

Titles of courses or subjects offered in school systems are often deceptive when transporting skills. They give the impression that programs offered in one system are unique from those offered in another school system. In fact, this is usually not the case, as is evident by the varied titles for the ninth grade "slow mathematics" required of all "terminal mathematics" students who must complete one Carnegie unit of high school mathematics credit prior to graduation. Such course titles as business mathematics, vocational mathematics, refresher mathematics, general mathematics, and host of others contain the same basic set of skills. A similar parallel exists in many English and social studies programs in school systems (for example, English Literature, Old World Literature, World Cultures, World History, World Problems).

Obviously there are programs that are not transportable. Locally designed and some state-mandated programs (North Dakota History, Indians of Minnesota, and West Virginia Studies to name a few) have little applicability if moved from their point of origination. Such programs do not exist to any great degree in school systems, however.

The issue of skill transportability may seem a moot point to the unwary. Most school systems do engage in a minimal amount of curriculum construction, test design, and diagnostic and placement work. Because skills are transportable, so too is most of the design work that school systems have undertaken to enhance the instruction of those skills. As school systems begin to recognize that their instructional programs are not totally unique from those of their neighboring systems, more extensive material sharing will take place and thus foster greater improvements in the learning options that can be provided to students and the resources available to teachers.

Examples and Parallels. Foundations for programs are more common in business, industry, and the professions than they are in the public or private education. In most of the cases illustrated below, the professions or endeavors have been far more completely identified than is customary in educational circles. Far less is left to chance or speculation. No judgments can be made on the quality of these foundations, but their wide use is suggestive of the significance they are accorded and the role they play in the conduct of quality programs or activities. The number of variables with which other professionals deal are at least equal to if not greater than that with which the teacher would be confronted.

- Foreman's procedures in maintaining an automotive assembly line
- Medical doctor's diagnostic procedure in identifying and treating illnesses
- Lawyer's strategy in preparing briefs for a case

- Professional football coach's practice and game strategy
- Carpenter's procedures in building a house
- Architect's procedures in building a hotel
- Mechanic's procedures in tuning-up a car
- Owner's procedures in training a race horse
- Coroner's strategy in conducting an autopsy
- Detective's strategy in solving a crime
- Farmer's procedures in raising a high yield crop
- Newsman's procedures in preparing a newspaper

In nearly every endeavor, there are definite skills, processes, and concepts that make up the foundation of that endeavor. The skills are essential to the mastery of that endeavor; without them the quality of the product produced will be substandard, or the diagnostic, placement, and prescriptive capacity needed to determine and mend product flaws will be unreliable. Instructional program foundations are basic to the operation of school systems and essential to the provision of appropriate instruction for all students. Without program foundations, school systems cannot guarantee instructional success.

Design Work for the Teacher

There are many activities related to instructional program foundation identification that the teacher can undertake alone if the school system is not disposed to do such valuable work. Before examining these, however, let us offer some precautionary advice.

Teachers will need to recognize that skill, concept, and process specification not done by the school system over fifty years of operation cannot be done in a few days nor can it necessarily be done perfectly. Bywords for your activities should include "patience" and "confidence." Take your time and be confident that what you are doing is better than nothing.

Try to enlist the help of all other teachers and the principal. If you cannot inspire everyone (and you may very well not be able to), work on those who teach the same course or grade level as you and, hopefully, those who teach courses or grade levels that precede and follow yours. For example, if you are a third grade teacher, try to enlist other third grade teachers and at least one second and one fourth grade teacher. If you are teaching at the secondary level, attempt to secure the teachers who instruct courses that are prerequisite to and, also, those that follow yours. Do not be surprised or dismayed if you find yourself in the role of Henny Penny.

With or without the assistance of others, precede in readying yourself for skill, concept, and process identification by securing general philosophy statements and program outcome statements or objectives that your school system may have developed. The school system policy manual is a good place to look, and it may generally be found in your building. This will not be a lot of help, but a five minute review may be somewhat enlightening. Also secure and review a curriculum guide (if one is available) for the course or program you are examining. An hour of research will tell something about the school system's program emphasis—classes of skills, skill mix, and skill relationships. It may further emphasize the importance of some of the skills, concepts, and processes in your program. Be sure to determine when the guide was developed and ask your principal whether or not its contents still apply (particularly if the school system has recently adopted new textbooks or a new philosophy dated after the curriculum guide's completion). Keep in mind that the curriculum guide, unless recently developed and excellently done, will rarely provide a detailed and accurate analysis of the instructional program foundation.

You are now ready to begin the analysis of the primary source documents available to you: the adopted textbook. When no other guidance is provided to direct instructional programs (curriculum guides, objectives, outcome statements), you must rely on the skill, concept, process content of the textbook. After all, under the above conditions, the textbook is the only instructional direction formally *adopted* by the board of education. In the event that later someone does not particularly like your work or is threatened by it, you can fall back on the fact that you merely identified or further specified works previously adopted by the board of education.

Page through the primary or basic text of the course or grade level you teach (elementary teachers will want to concentrate on only one program at a time—perhaps reading or mathematics). As you slowly examine the text, page by page, note the theme, focus, heading, or thrust *behind* the written word. Ask yourself constantly and persistently: "What is the author trying to get across here? What is this supposed to do? Where is this going?" Look at individual pages and then a span of pages to get the author's skill, concept, and process intent. After you have a feel for several pages, jot down in precise terms the skill, concept, or process that the written pages are designed to convey to the student. Use short, snappy phrases—not elaborate objectives or wordy, philosophical ramblings. Make certain you understand what you have written. Some skill examples are presented below and at the end of the chapter.

Visual discrimination of colors (reading)
Initial consonants: b, d, p, q (reading)
Solving quadratic equations (mathematics)
Climate and topography (geography)
Paragraph spacing (typing)
Boyle's and Charles' Laws (chemistry/physics)
Brush strokes: Six Types (art)
Adverbs: location and function (grammar usage)

A normal question that arises in skill, concept, and process identification is "how many skills are there?" The answer is a qualified, "it depends." If the reviewer over scrutinizes and lists skills, sub-classifications of skills and subclassifications of the sub-classifications, a three hundred page book can contain 2,000 skills. On the other hand, an under-classification of the same book may yield only ten skills, concepts, or processes. Because textbooks vary so much in content and depth, it is virtually impossible to give a reliable formula on how many skills, concepts, and processes a given book contains. Nonetheless, the teacher can gauge fairly accurately the skills normally taught and how many ought to be cited in the final program foundation. This can be done by considering the 180 day teaching pattern you employ. Ask yourself, in a given course or program, how often am I introducing a new skill (not a version of the one taught the day before) to my students. Such introspection normally causes an estimation of one skill (and variations of it) every three days to one every two days. Thus, as a focus to get started, try to identify sixty to ninety skills in the course or program, and make the skill name broad enough to include minor amplifications of the skill itself. By this latter point, it is suggested that the teacher may want to classify Birds of Minnesota, Birds of Kansas, Birds of North Dakota, and so forth under the broader skill, Birds of the Midwest, to reduce the number of skills, concepts, or process. However, teachers will want to avoid trying to reduce the number of skills on their list by classifying and grouping dissimilar skills under a common classification (classifying Birds of Minnesota, Birds of North Dakota, Aerodynamics of Flight, and Digestive Systems of Birds as Birds of the Midwest). Such misclassifications create problems in test design that can introduce substantial errors in student diagnosis and placement.

After sixty to ninety skills have been identified and written down, review the list and reclassify if it seems necessary or logical. It probably would be helpful to take a second paging through the book to affirm that there are no errors of omission. You may also want to write down the inclusive textbook page numbers where each skill is treated on the listing of skills, concepts, and processes that you have developed. This will be needed later.

With the instructional program foundation completed, you can review the classes of skills, skill mix, and skill relationships. It might be worth some time to write a "C" (for cognitive) alongside of those skills that are factually oriented (designed to provide facts or encourage factual mastery); an "A" (for affective) by those focusing on individual student or class attitude, value, or moral development; and a "P" (for psychomotor) by those designed to improve student motor skills. Now, you have completed the skill classification and can visualize the mix of skills. Do you need or want more factual, value, or motor emphasis in the program? If so, those skills, concepts, and processes should be added into the program foundation at appropriate points (or at the beginning of the foundation if they will be emphasized and assessed on a yearly basis). Take care to affirm that the newly included skills, concepts, and processes are not counter to the school system's philosophy or policies and that they do not cause the slighting or elimination of critical program skills.

Reviewing the logic and order of the instructional program foundation, it will be obvious what type of skill relationship exists in the program. This information will be helpful in later test construction.

In the event that the teacher is interested in pursuing further classifications of the skills, concepts, and processes and viewing the course or program in a different perspective, a summary or scope and sequence chart can be designed similar to the one at the end of the chapter. This document yields a picture of the curricula on a broad topical basis and is particularly effective for showing parents the continuity and breadth of a course or program. Incidentally, as teachers are developing instructional program foundations, they should be aware that textbook publishers' scope and sequence charts *are not* substitutes for identified and sequenced instructional program foundations, even though such charts are valuable for a teacher who is developing a foundation.

The experienced teacher who is using a basic textbook with which he is familiar can complete the tasks specified above in about ten hours. In some cases it will take longer, but the point is that the task is neither impossible nor endless. And the teacher must remember that the final product—no matter how seemingly unsophisticated—will be far more useful than that which generally exists in many school systems: nothing.

Presuming that you have undertaken these specification activities with other teachers, combine all of the work, review it, resolve inconsistencies, establish uniformity, and the basic program foundation is tentatively completed. Share it with your principal and colleagues and get their critical comment. After final revisions, you will be prepared to examine how the instructional program foundation plays a vital role in diagnosing students.

Documents

Two types of instructional program foundation examples are included on the following pages. First are sets of instructional program foundations for kindergarten-first grade social studies, kindergarten-first grade mathematics, second grade language usage, seventh grade life science, second year French, and office practice created by teachers in several school systems. All of them were identified from textual materials used by the teachers, and all represent a fine first attempt at local curriculum and foundation classification.

Each of the skill sequences incorporates those skills, processes, and concepts that school systems or their curriculum designers felt each student—capable of functioning at grade level—should acquire from the instructional program. Each skill sequence furnishes program direction; the capacity for diagnosis, placement, instruction/ prescription, and assessment; and a base for communication. Consequently, the identified and sequenced skills are instructional program foundations.

The second document is an instructional program summary chart for a K-6 language arts program. The purpose of the summary chart is to document the skills, concepts, and processes of an instructional program foundation by major themes or content strands. Such a chart aids in identifying recurring topics in a program, eliminating redundancies, ensuring desired skill emphasis or weighting, assessing skill balance by grade level, cross-referencing skills, and reviewing a number of less significant program features.

Though the documents are weighted slightly in favor of elementary school programs, it bears restatement that there are no structural differences between elementary and secondary school program foundations other than those enumerated previously. In fact, developing secondary school program foundations is a somewhat easier task to accomplish than at the elementary level where program correlation with many more programs is necessary and individualized instruction efforts prevail to a greater degree. The reason for selecting elementary school program foundations in greater numbers than secondary school ones is the tendency for the former to have undertaken skill identification more frequently than the latter.

Document 1
Sets of Instructional Program Foundations

K-1 SOCIAL STUDIES SKILLS

Develop an Awareness of Group Living within the School

Group Living—Identify Certain School Personnel

Group Living—Being Aware of Rules of School and Room

Group Living—Being Aware of Family Members

Family Structure

Family Structure—Living Quarters

Human Behavior—Child's Role in Relationship to Home

Family Living—Child's Role in the Family

Human Behavior—Child's Role in School

Environment

Human Behavior—Child's Role in the Community

Human Behavior—Child's Self-Concept

Safety at School and Home

Safety in the Community

Indian Life and Customs

Our Government

Community Helpers

Community—Public Buildings

Family Structure—Roles of Family

Family Structure—Types of Work

American Homes

American Homes—Purposes and Location

Homes—How They Differ

Farms

Animals Around Us

Manners at Home

Manners at School

Manners at Play

Safety at Home

Safety at School

Safety at Play

Safety During a Flood

Safety During a Tornado

Communication

Transportation

Maps and Globes

Holidays

Our Country—Patriotism and Freedom

Our Country—History

Our Country—Government

Our Country—Great Men

Our Country—Our Flag and Our Song

Alaska

Schools Around the World

K-1 MATHEMATICS SKILLS

Pre-readiness—set recognition

Recognition of geometric shape—circle

Recognition of the square

Recognition of triangles

Recognition of the rectangle

Recognition of geometric shapes

Developing visual memory and discrimination

Following directions

Ordering, classifying, and comparing sets

Positional and comparison relations

Spatial relationships

Thinking analytically and creatively about patterns

Introduction to comparing sets

One-to-one matching and equivalent sets

Nonequivalent sets and the concept of one more

Cardinal numbers and numerals 1 to 4

The number zero its numeral the empty set

Cardinal number and numeral 5

Cardinal number and numeral 6

Cardinal number and numeral 7

Cardinal number and numeral 8

Cardinal number and numeral 9

Cardinal number and numeral 10—counting and order 0 to 10

Sets and ideas related to subtraction (optional)

Money (optional)

Time (optional)

Measurement (optional)

Ordinals

Comparing sets—more, less

Equivalent sets

Sets with one more number

Numeration 1 to 4

Numeration 5 to 9

Value of penny—symbol ¢ for cent

Numeral writing

Ordering

"Greater than"—"less than" and the related inequality symbols

Union of sets, addition and the plus sign

Symbol for equality, equation, zero, and vertical notation

Missing addends in addition

Subtraction—minus symbol

Subtraction equations, vertical equations, subtractive property of zero in sums of five or less

Missing addends and sums in subtraction

Inverse relation—subtraction and addition with sums of five or less

Maintenance—addition combinations of five or less, introduction of addition combinations of six

Differences related to sums of six, number line in subtraction, and maintaining skills through practice with both plus and minus

Maintaining skill in addition combinations of six or less and introducing addition combinations of seven

Differences—sums of seven—maintaining skills and practice

Introduction of the nickel, application of addition and subtraction in working with coins

Maintenance of addition skills using combinations of seven or less and introduction for combinations of eight

Introduction of subtraction combinations related to sums of eight

Introduction of addition combinations of nine and maintaining skills through practice

Subtraction—sums of nine—maintaining skills through practice

Number and name for ten, grouping by tens, and sets of ten and more

Two-digit numerals—writing, meaning, and names—the decades

Order of numbers 0 to 99 and counting by decades

Progressing from one decade to the next and developing understanding of counting 0 to 99

Dimes, place value, maintenance of skills

Inequalities—the decades, within a decade, numbers from 0 to 99, and place value using coins

Telling time

Addition combinations of ten

Differences—sums of ten

Review of addition and subtraction using coins

Commutative principle

Review of sums of ten

The plus sign in place value

Grouping principle using the number line

Reasoning—sums greater than ten —three addends

Subtraction—sums greater than ten

Odd and even and skip counting

Fractions ½ and ⅓

Linear measure—inch and centimeter

Liquid measure

Geometric figures—triangle, circle, square, and rectangle

Number words and ordinals

GRADE 2 LANGUAGE USAGE SKILLS

Visual Impressions
Auditory Impressions
Sense of Taste
Sense of Smell
Sense of Touch
Review of Five Senses
Relativity of Perception
Classifying—several categories
Classifying—multiple character-
istics
Where, When, How
Inference through Sequencing
Inference and Knowledge
Similarities and Contrasts
Literature concerning Indians
Literature concerning Blacks
Poetry
Creative Dramatics

Punctuation—Exclamation Mark
Punctuation—Period (abbrevia-
tions)
Punctuation—Comma (cities,
states)
Punctuation—Comma (dates)
Capitalization—First Word (titles)
Capitalization—Mr.—Mrs.—Miss—
Dr.
Capitalization Names (streets)
Capitalization Names (tribes,
peoples, etc.)
Capitalization—review
Dictionary skills
Pronoun usage
Avoiding many "ands"
Verb endings ("s", "ed", "ing")

GRADE 7 LIFE SCIENCE

Introduction to Life Science: The
Tools of the Life Scientist—
Laboratory and Books
Introduction to Life Science: Life
Scientists
Awareness of Fresh Water Environ-
ments
Awareness of Marine Water En-
vironments
Factors that Affect the Environ-
ment: Land Community
Summative Test

The Cell: Structure and Parts
The Cell: Function and Processes
Summative Test

Taxonomy
Animals without Backbones:
Protozoa through Echinoderms

Animals without Backbones:
Annelida through Mollusca
Animals without Backbones: The
Arthropoda
Summative Test

Phylum Chordata: Early Chordates
through the Amphibians
Animals with Backbones: Reptiles,
Birds, and Mammals
Cells as a Part of Multicellular
Organisms
Awareness of Body Systems: Struc-
ture and Function of Skeletal,
Muscular, Digestive, and Nervous
Awareness of Body Systems: Struc-
ture and Function of Circulatory,
Respiratory, Excretory, Endo-
crine, and Reproductive
Summative Test

Photosynthesis: Chemical Equations and Respiration

The Thallophytes: Algae, Fungi, Lichens, and Bacteria

The Bryophytes: Mosses and Liverworts

The Ferns

Summative Test

The Structure and Function of the Leaf

The Structure and Function of the Stem

The Structure and Function of the Root

Summative Test

The Seed Plants: The Gymnosperms or Cone Bearers

The Seed Plants: Angiosperms with Two Seed Leaves, Angiosperms with One Seed Leaf

Summative Test

The Structure of a Flower: Parts, Reproduction and Meiosis

Pollination, Cross Pollination, and Vegetative Propagation

Summative Test

Heredity: Gregor Mendel, Walter Sutton and Their Work

Heredity: Genes in a Code

Summative Test

Changing Man and the Environment: Beginnings of Tribe, Town, and City

Conservation and Ecology: Man's Use and Misuse of the Environment

Conservation and Ecology: Modify-

ing the Environment and Wise Use of Ecosystems

Summative Test

Health and Nutrition: Four Basic Food Groups, Nutrients, and Calories

Health and Nutrition: Deficiency Diseases

Summative Test

Health and Diseases: Classification and Examples, Causes, and Germ Theory

Health and Disease Defenses: Immunity and Prevention

Summative Test

Health and Safety: Rules, Practices, and Procedures

Health and First Aid: Emergency Treatment

Health and Drugs: Proper Use and Misuse of Drugs

Health and Drugs: Drug Abuse and Causes of Abuse

Health and Drugs: Physical, Mental, and Social Effects of Drug Abuse

Health and Drugs: Legal Control

Summative Test

Health and Personal Hygiene

Body Systems of an Organism: The Frog

Heredity: Mutations, Case Studies, Theories

Changing Man and the Environment: Early Man, Artificial Selection, Man Changes the Environment

The Microscope: Parts, Use, Slides

FRENCH LEVEL II

Imperfect of *être,* Review of present *être*

Imperfect of *avoir,* Review of present *avoir*

Passé Composé—First conjugation verbs

Passé Composé—Irregular verbs

Adverbs—Placement and Formation from adjectives

Passé Composé—All conjugations

Imperfect Tense—State of Mind Verbs

Present tense—*venir, partir, sortir*

Passé Composé—verbs of movement (intransitive)

Future—*avoir, être*

Future—Irregular Verbs

Future—Regular Verbs

Direct and Indirect object pronouns

Pronouns: *y—en*

Double object pronouns in affirmative and negative statements

Use of irregular negatives

Irregular negatives (cont.)

Conditional—regular and irregular verbs

Conditional—Usage

Reflexive Verbs—Present

Reflexive Verbs—Past

Interrogative Pronouns

Interrogative Adjectives, Demonstrative Pronouns

Shopping

Literature

Sports

Letter Writing—French calendar

Telephone

Art and Music

Provinces and Departments

Paris

Other Cities

OFFICE PRACTICE

Math Review; Fundamental Processes; Addition and Subtraction

Math Review; Fundamental Processes; Multiplication and Division

Math Review; Computational Skills; Fractions

Math Review; Computational Skills; Decimals

Math Review; Computational Skills; Percentages

Math Review; Computational Skills; Interest

Math Review; Summative Post Test

Machines; Ten-key Adding Machine

Machines; Full-keyboard Adding Machine

Machines; Printing Calculator

Machines; Rotary Calculator

Machines; Key-driven Calculator

Machines; Electronic Calculator

Duplicating Methods; Stencil Process

Duplicating Methods; Fluid Process

Machines; Machine Transcription

Machines; Cash Register

Communications; Telephone

Business Letter Writing

Alphabetic Filing

Geographic, Numeric, and Subject
Filing

Filing Procedures and Equipment

Lester Hill Corporation Office
Simulation

How the Office is Organized

Career Possibilities

Evaluating Yourself

Getting the Job You Want

Cashiering Activities

Purchases and Accounts Payable

Inventory and Stock Systems

Sales Office Activities

Payroll Systems

Handling and Routing Mail

Offset Duplicating

Document 2
K–6 Summary Chart: Language Arts Program

LANGUAGE PERCEPTION:

Sensory Perception

Grade	
1	Perception of Self Perception of Others Perception of Surroundings
2	Visual Impressions Auditory Impressions Sense of Taste Sense of Smell Sense of Touch Review of Five Senses
3	Sense Perception
4	
5	
6	

Awareness of Language

Grade	
K	Vocabulary Development
1	Classifying (Introduction) Different names for one object Action Words Action words and name words Creative names and actions Need for Language
2	Relativity of Perception Classifying—Several Categories Classifying—Multiple Characteristics Where, When, How Similarities and Contrasts
3	Words as Symbols
4	
5	Shades of Meaning
6	Language and Symbol Classification and Continuum

LANGUAGE PRINCIPLES:

Capitalization and Punctuation		*Composition*	
1	Capital Letters Capitals—Pets' and People's Names Capitals—Word I Capitals—First word in sentence Capitals—Names and places Capitals—Weeks, Months and Holidays Review of Capitalization Period at end of sentence Question mark after question Period after initials	1	Five parts of the letter Letter writing, addressing envelopes Kinds of letters Form and unity in the paragraph Topic sentence in a paragraph
2	Capitals—Titles Capitals—Mr., Mrs., Miss, Ms., Dr. Capitals—Names of streets Capitals—Peoples, tribes, etc. Capitalization review Exclamation mark Period after abbreviations Comma between cities and streets Comma in dates	2	Paragraph as an idea unit Paragraph in time order Paragraph in space order Outlining
		3	Composition as an idea unit Composing titles Composition—Expanding Ideas Composition—Transitions Proofreading and rewriting

4	Newspaper Letter writing—friendly Letter writing—business Letter writing—post card Composing paragraphs Paragraphs, space order and time order Composition—unifying the idea Transitional phrases
5	Newspaper Note taking and summarizing Paragraph—Topic sentence Paragraph—Organizing Paragraph—Expanding and compressing Restricting the subject Unifying ideas Organizing ideas Transitional words or phrases Sensory impressions Proofreading and rewriting
6	

3	Commas in a series Contractions Titles of books, short stories, poems In letter writing Comma after yes and no in sentences Review—Capitalization & Punctuation
4	Capitalization of proper adjectives Periods in abbreviations Commas used in direct address Hyphen in syllable division Apostrophe to show possession Review
5	Capital review Punctuation review Comma usage Punctuation of direct quotation Use of colon
6	Capitalization review Punctuation review

Usage

1. Recognition of singular and plural words.

2. I and Me
Avoiding too many "*ands*"
Verb endings ("s", "ed", "ing")

3. Using the correct form of to, too, two
Using the correct form of there, their
Using the correct form of he, him, she, her
Prefixes, suffixes

4.

System of Language

1.

2.

3. Nouns
Verbs
Adjectives

4. Singular and plural nouns
Specific nouns
Specific verbs
Adjectives
Adverbs
Noun part—verb part

5

- Specific nouns
- Pronouns
- Specific verbs
- Adjectives and adverbs
- Verbs
- Noun part—verb part
- Compound sentences
- Complex sentences

6

- Specific nouns
- Pronouns
- Possessive pronouns
- Specific verbs
- Modifiers
- Compound sentences
- Complex sentences
- Prepositional phrases
- Sentence patterns

5

- Singular and plural verb endings
- Irregular verbs
- Main verbs and the helping verbs

6

- Subject-verb agreement

Literature

Grade	Poetry
K	Literature concerning Indians Literature concerning Blacks Poetry
1	For additional literature use Literary Enrichment Guide. Plan jointly with your librarian.
2	Literature concerning Indians Literature concerning Blacks Poetry
3	Literature concerning Indians Literature concerning Blacks Poetry
4	Literature concerning Indians Literature concerning Indians Literature concerning Blacks Poetry
5	Literature concerning Indians Literature concerning Blacks Poetry
6	Literature concerning Indians Literature concerning Indians Literature concerning Blacks Poetry

Inference

Grade	
1	
2	Inference through Sequencing Inference and Knowledge
3	Inference and Problem Solving
4	Inference and Evidence
5	Inference and Evaluation
6	Inference and Verification

Oral Language

Grade	Oral Language
K	Oral Communication; Listening and Storytelling; Dramatization; Experience Stories
1	Creative Dramatics
2	Creative Dramatics
3	Choral Reading
4	Tone of Voice, Pause, Stress, Pitch
5	Sender-Receiver; Medium-Message
6	Communication Activities

History of Language

Grade	History of Language
1	
2	
3	Origin and Meaning
4	Dialects
5	History of the Language
6	Origins of the English Language

Study Skills

Grade	
K	Alphabetical (ABC) Order
1	
2	Dictionary skills
3	Dictionary skills Using the table of contents and index Using the encyclopedia
4	Using the table of contents & index Syllabication
5	
6	

Creative Writing

Grade	
K–6	Creative writing is highly individualized and is recommended as a part of *the language program throughout the entire year in all grades.* Teachers are expected to incorporate their own ideas and performance criteria in this area.
2	Expressing feelings or point of view Imaginative writing
3	Using metaphor and simile Using sensory impressions
4	
5	Creative writing ideas (This package might be useful at other grade levels as well.)
6	Writing a Storybook

3.   Diagnosis

Diagnosis is the procedure used to determine a student's readiness for learning within the school system's instructional program foundation. It is an examining process—one that yields a status report on those skills, concepts, and processes that a student has mastered, exhibits questionable mastery, and displays deficiency. The desired purposes of instructional diagnosis are the successful placement and instruction of the student.*

The Values of Instructional Diagnosis

The first formal instructional picture that educators obtain of their students is through instructional diagnosis. Diagnosis may be a detailed review of a student's anecdotal and academic history, observation, parental and student interviews, formal testing, or any combination of these procedures. Whichever one or ones are used, however, it is certain that accurate and specific data must be gathered if the teacher is to place and instruct the student successfully.

*The author wishes to recognize the invaluable assistance of Dr. Catherine Candor, Director of Research and Evaluation, Kanawha County Schools, Charleston, West Virginia, for her creative assistance in detailing the contents and procedures of this chapter. Miss Candor is particularly congratulated for her seminal efforts in criterion-referenced test construction in the aforementioned school district.

It is not uncommon for student diagnosis to be poorly executed. Faulty diagnosis may be caused by (1) poor identification of instructional program foundations, (2) a failure to tie test results to instructional program content, (3) diagnostic instruments whose content and emphases conflict with local program content, (4) inadequate staff understanding of diagnostic test content and meaning, (5) a failure of tests to pinpoint the differences between critical and insignificant skill deficiencies to teachers, or (6) faulty interpretation and application of test data in placing and instructing the student. Faulty diagnosis can have a profound influence on whether or not students and local instructional programs will succeed or fail. Because placement and instruction are directly dependent upon diagnosis, the more poorly diagnosis is carried out the greater is the probability that students will be taught at some point other than where they should be functioning. In turn, this increases the probability that students will fail to acquire instructed skills, concepts, and processes.

Accurate diagnosis furnishes educators with a wealth of information about students, instructional program content, and personnel effectiveness. Among the most significant values of sound diagnosis are information tendered about (1) student skill deficiencies, (2) placement indicators, (3) instructional foundation deficiencies, (4) program gaps, (5) program articulation, (6) inservice training needs, and (7) instructional effectiveness.

Student Skill Deficiencies. The most valuable information that diagnosis provides is the identification of those skills that students can and cannot perform. When that information is compared to the school system's program foundation, teachers are able to make tentative judgments about the location, magnitude, and probable cause of students' learning problems. Depending upon the combination of skill problems identified, they can also predict the rate with which learning problems can be corrected and the long-range learning goals that can reasonably be accomplished by the student.

Placement Indicators. Diagnosis aids teachers in determining where students should be located in a program foundation to maximize learning. While diagnosis provides indications of learning weakness, it also furnishes valuable information on previous skills acquired. Instructional placement is generally selected at a point just beyond skills where students have demonstrated mastery but prior to skills where they have shown learning weakness or nonmastery. Correct placement may be identified as the position in the program foundation where students will be able to use skills that were previously learned as a base for understanding and acquiring skills, concepts, and processes that are to follow.

Instructional Program Foundation Weaknesses. Weaknesses in instructional program foundations are periodically identified through student diagnosis. Among the more frequent weaknesses exposed are the illogical ordering of skills (a set of closely related skills containing one or more very unrelated ones), the inclusion of unnecessary skills, the illogical sequencing of skills (simple skills followed by complex skills followed by simple skills), and the usage of excessive random skill relationships that prevent students from applying earlier learning to present learning and prohibit the teacher from making judgments about student placement.

Typically, program foundation weaknesses are identified by the bizarre performances large numbers of students exhibit on diagnostic tests. For example, test results may illustrate alternating correct and incorrect responses to test questions that would make the teacher think students could not perform simple skills correctly but could, miraculously, show mastery on more difficult ones requiring a knowledge of those simpler skills. The following student performance on a diagnostic test is indicative of an instructional program foundation that has been poorly constructed and sequenced:

Skill 1	−	
Skill 2	+	
Skill 3	+	
Skill 4	−	*+ Indicates correct response*
Skill 5	+	*− Indicates incorrect response*
Skill 6	−	
Skill 7	−	
Skill 8	+	
Skill 9	−	
Skill 10	+	

The identification of instructional program foundation weaknesses has positive implications for the improvement of a school system's programs. Many times it suggests more logical patterns of arranging skills, identifying areas in which the instructional foundation's skills, concepts, and processes can be pruned, and establishing a need for constantly updating and justifying content. Diagnosis assists in making instructional programs more easily understandable to both the teacher and the student and insures that program logic is encouraging and not working against student learning.

Program Gaps. Diagnosis can provide valuable data on unintended gaps that exist in programs. Commercial publishing firms and educators make certain assumptions about the ability of students to transfer or apply prior learning to more difficult learning tasks. Unfortunately, there are times when commercial materials overestimate the breadth of a student's ability to apply earlier learning to a new task, and the transition from one skill to the next is poorly structured. Thus, one finds gaps in the program foundation that are significant enough to cause even the best student to fail. The following diagnostic results are indicative of what can be expected when using curricular materials that have program or skill gaps:

Skill Sequence:	A	B	C	D	H	I	J	+ *Indicates correct*
Student A	+	+	+	+	−	−	−	*response*
Student B	+	+	+	+	−	−	−	− *Indicates incorrect*
Student C	+	+	+	+	−	−	−	*response*

Though the previous instructional program foundation was designed to illustrate a logical sequence of closely related skills, obviously that goal was not realized. Some vehicle is needed to aid students in making the transition from skill D to H. Either additional skills need to be inserted in the instructional foundation, the instructional units used to teach skills H, I, and J must be simplified or better correlated, or a stronger relationship (perhaps aided by varied methodological approaches) between skills D and H will need to be reinforced. Whatever approach is finally selected, program gaps can be minimized if they are identified through student diagnosis, smoothed out, and repeatedly checked through further diagnosis.

Program Articulation. Diagnosis furnishes the capability to locate points in programs where there is inadequate articulation or instructional follow-up. For example, special care needs to be exercised in diagnosing students as they make the transition from one grade or school level to the next. Too often, it is assumed that students are prepared for instruction at a certain grade level because they have been promoted, their report cards seem to reflect readiness for the higher grade level, or simply because of their chronological ages. Using this logic, students are automatically placed at the beginning point of the grade level's skill content without any diagnosis of skill strengths or weaknesses.

Frequently diagnostic testing illustrates that students will have problems in grade or school level articulation unless special program adjustments are made. Diagnosis may depict that previous grade level instruction has not provided the range of requisite skills, concepts, and processes some students need to succeed at a higher grade level. It also delineates those preplacement skill weaknesses that cause students problems in making satisfactory progress in subsequent learning activities. Finally, it may well show that instruction in the previous grade level did not progress to the point higher grade level teachers normally would have assumed. In all of these instances, students will have problems with articulation unless diagnosis precedes placement and instruction.

Diagnostic data propose to foster smooth program articulation by exposing those skills that students have not mastered or to which they have not been introduced. These skills, concepts, and processes will require careful attention by the teacher if subsequent instruction is to be effective. The problem of grade or program articulation

Fig. 1
Program Articulation

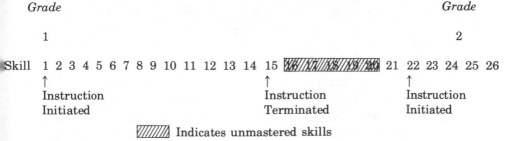

Grade   *Grade*

1   2

Skill 1 2 3 4 5 6 7 8 9 10 11 12 13 14 15 ▨▨▨▨▨ 21 22 23 24 25 26
       ↑   ↑   ↑
       Instruction   Instruction   Instruction
       Initiated   Terminated   Initiated

       ▨▨▨ Indicates unmastered skills

(see figure 1) is one that will be pointed out by sound diagnosis and can be alleviated by subsequent correct placement and instruction.

Inservice Training Needs. Diagnostic data gathered on school system students can serve as a basis for inservice training programs and curriculum design sessions. Skill deficiencies commonly exhibited by students, placement problems and procedures, program articulation problems, and program gaps are topics whose analysis can greatly increase the effectiveness of classroom instruction and, as such, their examination is particularly appropriate for teacher inservice training. In the same manner, these topics are central considerations for the analysis and reformulation of curricular programs. There is no better basis for training and development efforts than to consider actual student deficiencies, programming flaws, and instructional unit weaknesses in the school system that are exposed through sound diagnostic testing. The study of such problematical areas invariably leads to the suggestion of alternative program foundations, content, methodological procedures, or organizational patterns that hold promise for increased student learning.

Instructional Effectiveness. Student diagnostic test data provide educators with valuable information about the effectiveness of classroom instruction. Used at the beginning of and following instruction, diagnostic tests can illustrate the soundness of various staff, organization, scheduling, and methodological patterns used in instruction. They can also pinpoint faulty diagnosis, placement, and instruction procedures employed by staff members. They are able to demonstrate whether or not judiciousness was employed in the selection of instructional materials and the degree to which students were furnished with needed individual attention.

The examination of instructional effectiveness is the one value of instructional diagnosis educators most ignore or least often use. Obviously, the reason for such an attitude is the certainty that better student diagnosis will expose occasional teacher inadequacies. This is to be expected, and it should not be avoided. Teachers will be aware that the same principles of diagnosis and problem correction applied to students are also effective for teachers, and the identification and elimination of teaching deficiencies are positive steps toward improved teaching performance. This, in turn, can lead to improved student learning. To ignore substandard instruction without any attempts to remediate it is to court failure for both the teacher and his students.

Designing Effective Instructional Diagnostic Systems

Effective instructional diagnostic systems are not readily available in most school systems in the United States. This occurs, in part, because school system administrators and teachers have rarely felt qualified or comfortable conducting research and evaluation activities. At the same time, a spate of commercial testing and evaluation firms have had test instruments available that could be reasonably obtained and, presumably, provided the type of service that school systems needed. Until recently, educators have been comfortable with this seemingly successful symbiotic relationship. Now, however, they are questioning the ability of commercial diagnostic tests to provide the specific qualitative data that are necessary to carry out school programs and make effective instructional decisions. For the first time, they are beginning to brush up on methodological procedures for designing their own instructional diagnostic systems.

The impetus for this change came from two flaws in commercially produced tests: their data were too hard to interpret, and they were not easily related to instructional materials used in the local school district. Because of the intricate data maze that principals, teachers, and parents had to study to understand and apply information from commercial tests and the difficulty they have had trying to justify test results, only the barest data have been used in the most superficial ways. Even then, on more than one occasion administrators and teachers have found themselves in a difficult position trying to explain a student's test score or his instructional placement position to a parent.

The recent popularization of criterion-referenced tests has provided new diagnostic possibilities for school systems and encouraged more of them to consider designing their own instruments for instructional diagnosis. Criterion-referenced tests are instruments constructed on the basis of the unique program foundations identified in a local school system. They are used to determine program and student performances in a school system with relationship to goals, objectives, and program foundations that have been set locally. As such, criterion-referenced instruments aid a school system in accurately assessing the degree to which it has accomplished the goals it has set for itself.

Unlike commercially designed tests, locally developed criterion-referenced tests have a direct relationship with the skill content of local programs. The content of these tests parallels the content taught in the classrooms. Numerous advantages occur as a result: all data gathered from the tests are directly related to the instructional programs; all data have instant applicability for diagnosis, placement, and instruction without confusing or complex interpretation; all data can be used for comparing the quality of similar programs found in the school system; all data reflect the school system's instructional priorities—insuring that the format of test items, skill sequence, skills included, and those not included are actually as they appear in a program under study. Additionally, the usual disclaimers leveled at commercially prepared tests ("We don't teach these skills; they don't test *our* skills; the item format is different and confuses our students; we teach these skills at a different grade level; the tests' priorities aren't the same as ours; the information is not of value to me; it doesn't apply to my students.") are not applicable in school systems that have constructed and are using local criterion-referenced tests.

The implications of a criterion-referenced test design are far reaching. The tests are capable of highly effective diagnosis. They have the capacity to pinpoint instructional placement. They can identify recurring student performance inconsistencies that disclose instructional foundation deficiencies, program gaps, articulation faults, curriculum construction and inservice training needs, and instructional ineffectiveness. In substance, criterion-referenced tests furnish an encompassing quantitative and qualitative picture of school systems' instructional programs when compared to standards that the community, board of education, administration, and teaching staff have set for students and programs.

Designing an effective diagnostic system is a task whose difficulty is directly related to a school system's commitment to undertake program foundation identification and its belief in the need for accurate diagnosis. If either of these ingredients is absent, it is a waste of time to attempt criterion-referenced test design. At the same time, school system size, the absence of local research and evaluation personnel, and no past experience in designing diagnostic systems should not influence educators' thinking about whether or not they can develop a sound diagnostic system. Administrators in smaller school systems need not feel that their system's size or lack of specialized evaluation personnel will militate against their completion of an effective system. In fact, school systems with minimal course offerings and smaller enrollment have an advantage of being able to design and implement a diagnostic system in a shorter period of time than large, metropolitan school systems that are often hampered by inertia. On the other hand, larger school systems generally have more personnel who have the expertise to produce elaborate test forms, diagnostic analyses, and information reports than do smaller school systems. Larger school systems are usually far slower to implement new techniques on a generalized basis than are smaller systems, however, and they must spend substantially larger amounts of time attending to staff misunderstanding and misuse of the final products. Nonetheless, there is no reason why any school system—regardless of its size—cannot successfully design an accomplished diagnostic system that will furnish necessary and accurate data with which to make sound instructional decisions.

The tasks involved in developing an instructional diagnostic system are nearly identical in all school systems. Basic to each system are (1) specification of program skills, (2) development of test items, (3) development of test item pools, (4) referencing test items to program content, (5) cross-referencing program skills, (6) construction of the basic test, (7) conduct of a pilot test, (8) completion of final test revision, and (9) conduct of student diagnosis.

Specification of Program Skills. The key in the design of any instructional diagnostic system and in all criterion-referenced test construction is the specification of program skills, concepts, and processes. In the same manner that program foundations set the instructional direction and content sequence in classrooms, they are the basis for developing instructional diagnostic systems.

Criterion-referenced tests are built around the actual program skills taught in a school system. If skills, concepts, and processes have not been identified and are not certified as basic to a school system's instructional programs, tests will have to be developed on a "best guess" basis of what is "believed" to be the school system's skills. If the assumed or guessed skills do not, in fact, match the school system's actual program skills (as taught in the classroom) then the tests developed from them will not be criterion-referenced, will not be valid, and will have less diagnostic accuracy and placement value than if the tests were truly criterion-referenced.

School systems that have not previously specified skills will need to undertake the process of tentative and final skill identification (see chapter 2). Those that have completed this task for their programs and courses will be able to begin the process of refining their skills. It will be necessary that educators affirm that their skills represent the totality of that which is to be acquired by the student in each program or course. They will also need to be viligant in removing superficial and repetitive skills.

In the first attempts at skill identification, educators will identify a prodigious number of skills, often including subcategorizations of skills. This is to be expected and in many instances, leads to the development of diagnostic instruments that have a finer capacity to pinpoint student strengths and weaknesses. Those school systems that identify only a meager number of program skills increase the chances that their instruments will do less well in producing accurate diagnostic and placement data.

The final sets of program skills, concepts, and processes identified by a school system are the determiners of the eventual content of criterion-referenced tests. Therefore, the program skills should be refined to a point that can meet the following characteristics:

- Represent the total focus of the program or course.
- Are considered imperative for the attainment of school system or program goals, objectives, and results.
- Are stated in precise terminology (which may or may not be readily understandable to the noneducator).
- Are stated concisely.
- Are stated in the sequence most commonly used in classroom instruction.
- Represent a desired mix of skill classes.
- Represent the community's desires and expectations.

Development of Test Items. A second task in constructing an effective instructional diagnostic system is the development of test items that will make up the final instruments. Test items are developed for each skill included in each program or course under consideration.

Criterion-referenced test items can take almost any form: multiple choice, matching, open-ended, fill-in-the-blank, diagramming, and others. Test items can be empirically developed; revisions of items taken from school system textual materials; revisions of items taken from textual or supplemental resources available from other commercial materials; or items gathered from commercial or school system test item banks. However they are selected, they must match the skills that the school system has identified as a part of its instructional program foundations.

Special care must be taken to insure that the format for items, the terminology of test instructions to the student, item wording, and information requested to answer items are not confusing to the student and do not vary from what one would commonly find used in classroom instruction. Otherwise, it is conceivable that students will fail to demonstrate a knowledge of skills tested because of misunderstanding the directions or the information requested rather than an inability to compute the correct answers. If the former occurs, diagnostic and placement data will be inaccurate. In these instances, teachers will have gathered data illustrating students' weaknesses in "test taking" that may have no relationship to student difficulties in problem solving.

At least one test item (and preferably three or more) should be constructed or selected for each program or course skill. The items will need to be carefully examined to insure that they are appro-

Fig. 2
Criterion-Referenced Test Items

Skill: Visual Discrimination
Directions: Put an "X" on the square.
Item: □ ○ △ □

Skill: Visual Discrimination
Directions: Put an "X" on the letter which is the same as the letter in the box. (Show the students the letter in the box).
Item: M̄   M   W   N   Z
Skill: Two digit subtraction without regrouping
Directions: Subtract the following problems.
Item: 37
      -24

Skill: Acids and Bases
Directions: Identify which of the following is (are) acid(s).
         a. $NaHCO_3$
         b. $HC_2H_3O_2$
         c. $NaOH$
         d. $Ca(OH)_2$
         e. None of these

priate to the skills they are assessing. Where more than one item is used to assess skill acquisition, items may vary in structure and content as long as the directions for answering them are not ambiguous or unable to be interpreted by students.

The quality of test items developed is difficult to assess until students have actually taken the completed criterion-referenced tests. At that time, further analysis and revision is generally warranted to extract invalid, ambiguous, and extraneous items. Figure 2 illustrates examples of criterion-referenced test items and the skills that they are designed to assess.

Development of Test Item Pools. School system personnel may find it beneficial to develop many test items or pools to measure the acquisition of each program or course skill rather than developing only a few for each skill. The availability of a pool of test items gives a school system the latitude to construct multiple forms of desired tests or ones that have many items representing each skill.

Large collections of test items also provide the backup that is necessary for later replacing items that turn out to be invalid, confusing, or poorly constructed in trial testing. These items will need to be removed before final test forms are published, and it can be costly—in time and money—to reconstitute a test item writing team to develop needed replacement items.

Finally, test item pools offer a school system a broader range of item types from which to draw. Writing teams that develop only a few items for each skill may tend to stereotype them; this is less likely to occur if a multitude of items are written for each skill by several different writers.

Referencing Test Items to Program Content. A crucial task in the design of an effective diagnostic system is referencing test items to program content. Because a primary purpose of criterion-referenced testing and general diagnosis is to determine textual and other materials into which students will be placed after their learning problems are identified, it is imperative that some means be made available for the teacher to connect test data to instructional content. The identification of student deficiency is, in itself, of minimal value to the teacher. But, the link between data illustrating student learning weaknesses and program content that can alleviate those weaknesses is critical to the teacher. Referencing test items to program content provides this information.

Referencing begins with the listing of skills, concepts, and processes for a program or course. Each skill's location is determined, and the book and page number(s) where it may be found in the school system's texts and other materials are cited. Subsequently, test items developed for each skill are coded with the same book and page number references that are ascribed to the skill. These simple reference notations permit the teacher to identify the location of instructional content (books and page numbers) that treat any particular skill on which students have demonstrated problems in testing. The referencing process hastens the location of appropriate instructional materials and increases the speed and accuracy of student placement. Figure 3 is a sample of test item to program content referencing.

Fig. 3
Content Referencing

Skill: Visual Discrimination
Program Content Reference: Houghton-Mifflin, Level 1, pp.14–27
pp.33–37
Holt, Rinehart, Winston, Level 1, pp.5–9
pp.17–22
Test Item: Put an "X" on the square. HM-1 (14–27; 33–37)
□ ○ △ □ HRW-1 (5–9; 17–22)

Cross-Referencing Program Skills. Most instructional programs contain skills that have dependency relationships with other skills. In other words, there are some skills that are acquired only after or as a result of mastering a series of simpler, related skills. For example, it is improbable that a student will master the addition of select two digit numerals (27 + 15) until he has mastered the addition of one digit numerals (7 + 5), maintaining, carrying, and the concept of ten skills. Where dependency relationships exist among skills, it is valuable for the teacher to be able to identify both a student's skill weaknesses *and* other skills of dependency that may have contributed to the weaknesses exposed on the test. Cross-referencing program skills is designed to give the teacher access to this type of information.

Cross-referencing begins with the listing of instructional skills, concepts, and processes for a program or course. Then, content for each skill is reviewed to determine those skills that have dependency relationships. Clusters or groups of skills that are hierarchically or cyclically arranged and characterized by a relatively definite sequence, progressively more difficult skills, and a required mastery of earlier skills before students are introduced to more difficult skills are sources where skill dependency relationships are located. (Dependent skills are found both within grade level programs, particularly hierarchical and cyclical programs, and between grade levels.) After the dependency relationships have been identified among skills, each skill is assigned a number* that is unique to that skill. That number is subsequently attached to any other skill whose mastery is dependent upon the earlier skill. Each skill has other skills referenced to it and, in turn, is referenced to other skills unless it has no dependency to or with other skills. It is indeed unusual that educators would find more than a few skills without dependency relationships.

In school systems where program skills are cross-referenced, criterion-referenced tests are developed, and test items and program content are referenced, the classroom teacher will be able to use diagnostic test results to identify (1) student skill weaknesses, (2) the location of content materials appropriate to the skills where problems were exhibited, (3) dependent skills related to the skill weaknesses, and (4) the location of content appropriate to each of the dependent skills.

A sample program skill cross-reference is detailed below:

Skill:	Addition of Two Digit Numbers	MA 151-175.00**
Cross-Reference:	Maintenance, Addition Combinations of Five or Less	MA 151-165.00
	Maintenance, Addition Combinations of Four or Less	MA 151-155.00
	Missing Addends in Addition	MA 151-150.00
	Union of Sets	MA 151-145.00
	Greater than, Less than, Equal to	MA 151-140.00
	Ordering	MA 151-130.00
	Numeration 5-9	MA 151-125.00
	Numeration 1-4	MA 151-120.00

*A typical numbering system that may be used for classifying skills by grade level and sequence is illustrated on pages 82 to 85. Such a numbering system can be of assistance to teachers in coding and locating both program skills and materials.

**The numbers used to denote the skill and cross references were derived from the numbering system to page 82 to 85.

Construction of the Basic Test. In developing an effective diagnostic system, constructing the criterion-referenced test instrument is the culminating activity. It follows skill, concept, and process identification, test item development, test item pool construction, and test item and program skill referencing. The sophistication and quality of these earlier tasks will determine the accuracy and value of the data that will be garnered from the basic and final test forms.

Procedures for criterion-referenced test construction will vary from one school system to the next according to the desires of school personnel and the anticipated outcomes expected from the test. Every school system, however, will examine a number of common design components in arriving at their first basic test. The key components that will be considered are (1) grade level span of the test; (2) number of skills in the test; (3) number of items for each skill; (4) duration of the test; (5) format of items; (6) test directions; (7) answer sheets; and (8) information to be reported.

The number of grade levels a test spans will affect the number of skills in the test, items allotted to assess each skill, and the test duration. The broader is the grade level span of a test the more general will be the diagnostic information received and the greater are the chances of making errors in judging students' performances and placement. Both diagnostic and assessment tests should have a grade level span of at least one year and should be able to be pieced together with higher and lower level tests to furnish a testing continuum that extends from the beginning to the end of the range of program skills *without skill or item duplication.* Tests used primarily for placement will be of greater value to teachers if they are constructed to assess skills from the midpoint of the grade level below through the midpoint of the grade level above the grade level the teacher is instructing. Thus, teachers will find it beneficial to have a test that includes skills from grades three and one-half through four and one-half to assess students entering fourth grade. More usable skill placement data will be obtained from this test than from a grade four test. After all, most students entering fourth grade after a summer's vacation normally would do very poorly on a grade four test, which contains virtually no skills to which the students have been exposed. Using the grade four test, the teacher would obtain nearly no diagnostic profile on any of the students and, hence, would be unable to effect placement on the basis of mastered and unmastered skills. With a three and one-half to four and one-half test, teachers will obtain a sound diagnostic profile on most of their students. Generally, however, the classroom teacher will need to administer lower level tests (two and one-half to three and one-half grade skill span) and higher level tests (four and one-half to five and one-half grade skill span) to determine placement of some of the students in the class. This will occur because it is unlikely that all students will have the capability to function in instructional programs within a one grade level range. In this instance, it will be necessary to determine where the remaining students will be placed.

The number of skills contained in a criterion-referenced test will be dependent upon the grade level span of the test and the number of skills identified within the grade level span. Tests should be developed to assess a span of at least one grade level. They can span more if the time for administering them does not become too long and each skill is still represented well enough with test items. Diagnostic and placement tests with skill content of less than one year are unnecessarily inefficient and may require that several tests need to be administered to ascertain beginning student placement in just one grade level or course.

Generally speaking, all skills within the span of the test should be represented on the test. Obviously, if the test span is too great this is not possible, and test developers may want to eliminate dependent or lower level skills ·and emphasize only higher order or more encompassing skills to reduce the test's size and the duration of administration (one digit numeral addition skill, 7 + 6 and two digit numeral addition skill, 17 + 16 are eliminated from the test content and are encompassed within the three digit numeral addition skill, 127 + 116). When this is done, however, items answered incorrectly are not explicit in identifying the location of student problems, inasmuch as any of the three skills above encompassed by a test item may have caused an incorrect response. Such multiskill items may generally require additional testing by the teacher and are consequently less efficient for diagnostic and placement purposes. If possible, efforts should thus be made to test each skill or, certainly, each important one individually.

The number of items established for the assessment of each skill in a criterion-referenced test is dependent upon the degree of confidence that educators wish to have in predicting a student's ability or inability to show mastery of a skill. The greater the number of test items included for each skill the greater is the diagnostic accuracy. At the same time, as the number of items for each skill increases, the time involved in test administration increases and the grade level span or number of skills must decrease. Some compromise must be achieved, and educators generally will insert a sufficient number of items for each skill to yield a "reasonable picture" of skill acquisition. Generally speaking, one item for each skill is too few (a correct or incorrect answer on one item is not indicative of mastery or nonmastery); two items can be questionable (one item correct and one incorrect is inconclusive); but three items yield fairly conclusive evidence (three items correct is excellent evidence of mastery; two correct or two incorrect items are strong evidence of mastery or nonmastery; and three items incorrect are excellent evidence of nonmastery). Obviously, increasing the number of items beyond three for each skill further increases the predictability of diagnostic results; but time and test span become increasingly bigger problems.

The time required for test administration is a critical issue in test construction. Long tests can have a significant effect on student performance and, as a consequence, yield questionable or inaccurate diagnostic results. Testing time is affected by several variables, among which the following play the most prominent roles: the student's age; the grade level span; the number of skills; the number of items for each skill; the complexity of the questions and expected responses (format of items); and conditions of testing. Teachers will want to vary the time span for testing students of different ages, recognizing that tolerance and attention decline rapidly as tests are administered to younger students. At the same time, it must be recognized that tests can be administered in successive time periods, on successive days, or with varied formats to maintain student interest and alertness. These variations are far superior to reducing test size or the number of skills tested to a point where the data gathered are so scanty and general that the diagnostic potential of the test is lost.

Perhaps there are no two more important functions performed in educational programs than student diagnosis and placement, and educators must guard to insure that these functions are performed in a superior manner, even if a few extra hours or days of testing is required. Two or three days "lost" to diagnostic testing may well save some students from failing or doing very poorly for 180 days. As a general practice, test designers would do well to determine the information that is desired to accomplish meaningful diagnosis and placement and, then, determine testing time. Considering the age of the students taking the test, administration can be scheduled for as many time periods as is necessary to collect the quantity of data needed to insure accurate diagnosis and placement.

Test items of different format or style can be used in criterion-referenced instruments, but it is important for teachers to note that the choice of formats may have a significant impact upon the accuracy of diagnostic data gathered and the methods employed in test correcting. Item formats that require a series of steps for students to produce a correct response or cause them to copy or transpose information from one form to another may cause younger students to respond incorrectly when they are actually proficient in a skill. (This is particularly true when early elementary school students are asked to respond to multiple choice questions or transfer answers from a test form to computer cards.) In other instances some test items heighten diagnostic error by encouraging guessing that might be accurate (true-false and multiple choice items with only a few answer choices). A semi-related but important consideration in selecting the format of test items is whether or not tests will be hand or machine scored. Tests requesting open-ended responses (fill-in-the-blank, essay, matching columns) require hand scoring while other limited-response items (crossing, underlining, or circling the correct response) can either be hand or machine scored. Though these are seemingly mundane issues, they should be considered early in the process of test development to insure that the district has deployed people or machinery to the correction task. Regardless of the mode of test correction, it is vital that receiving diagnostic information not become slowed to a point where it is either so frustrating or illtimed that it is no longer of value to teachers. Test items and answer sheets developed in the appropriate format can, of course, be machine scored using an optical scanner or computer to speed the results on to the teacher.

Both accuracy of diagnostic data and rapid return of data are important considerations for classroom teachers. As such, school systems will generally use a combination of test item formats that necessitate more than one form of test correction to achieve desired ends. Most often they will employ limited response items for younger students, which are answered directly on test documents by circling answers. These will generally require hand scoring or keypunching before final test results can be computed. For older students, limited response items with open-ended options (Select the correct answer: a. 5; b. 15; c. 18; d. 20; e. None of these) can be used to minimize guessing. These answers can be placed directly onto computer cards for machine processing with no intermediary steps or they can be scored with correcting machines or overlay answer keys.

Directions on test procedures and responding to test items need to be carefully stated and provided with appropriate illustrative examples to insure understanding. Careful pruning of jargon and an avoidance of unfamiliar or confusing terminology are vital. Directions should be as standard as possible and avoid abrupt changes in the types of responses required of the student (Question 1: Put an X on the correct answer; Question 2: Circle the correct answer; Question 3: Put an X on the correct answer). As a basic principle, directions and procedures should be simply worded, detailed and illustrated, and free of the assumption that there are points that can be left to the imagination of the test administrator or taker.

Answer sheets are generally selected or developed to fit the manner in which the tests will be corrected by the school system. Obviously, they will also need to be coordinated with the format of test items and the test directions and procedures. In some instances, responses to test items are recorded directly onto the test form or booklet, and there is little probability for misinterpretation about where answers are to be recorded. Other answer sheets are distinct from the test form (mark cards, optical scan sheets, and so forth). The usage of these must be explained with the same simple, yet detailed, illustrations that characterize directions given to students on testing procedures and answering test items.

Constructing criterion-referenced tests necessitates an examination of the information to be reported for diagnosis. All information that may be desired by teachers from the diagnostic testing will need to be specified in the test before it is designed, and steps will need to be taken to insure that the data can and will be acquired in usable form. Some of the diagnostic information teachers may wish to obtain are (1) item response, (2) skill strands, (3) item references, (4) skill cross references, (5) skill class, and (6) placement. Information pertinent to these six issues can be developed onto test forms that are to be hand corrected or programmed into a computer. In either case, through preplanning, the classroom teacher can obtain far more explicit diagnostic data on a student than the mere indication of a correct or incorrect response to a test item. Each of the above areas of information are briefly described below and a typical example of data that could be provided to teachers on a given test item is illustrated.

- Item Response—Indicates whether or not the test item was answered correctly or incorrectly by the student.
- Skill Strands—Indicates whether or not a specific skill is part of a skill group and identifies the name of the skill group.
- Item Reference—Specifies the skill and test item number (if each item for that skill was numbered to coincide with the skill it tested) and distinguishes it from other items relating to the same skill. This is particularly valuable in determining the validity of a particular test item when many items are being evaluated on their ability to assess a skill.
- Skill Cross References—Specifies numbers of other skills which are related to the skill in question and have a dependency relationship with the skill.
- Skill Class—Specifies toward which class of skills (cognitive, affective, psychomotor) the item and skill is directed.
- Placement—Specifies whether or not the student's instructional placement should begin at this skill.

Skill: Addition of Digits of 4 or less

Skill Number: MA 151-030.00

Item 10: Add and find the sum of $\begin{array}{r} 4 \\ +3 \\ \hline \end{array}$ Ans. 7

• Response:	Incorrect
• Skill Strand:	Arithmetic Computation
• Item Reference:	MA 151-130.00 − 7
• Skill Cross References:	MA 151-125.00
	MA 151-120.00
	MA 151-105.00
	MA 151-095.00
• Skill Class:	Cognitive
• Placement:	No placement

Though processing diagnostic information can be substantially more rapid when it is produced by a computer, it can be obtained in school systems that do not have data processing equipment. All of the information required for the six categories above must be determined by humans before the content of a test is complete. Owning a computer does not reduce the time taken to complete these tasks. From that point on, the school system not owning a computer can place or print item data (skill strand, item reference, skill cross reference, and skill class) directly onto the test form or booklet adjacent to test items. Though hand correction of responses and mentally establishing the point of student placement is necessary, the identical diagnostic data will be available to the school system that has no computer as well as to the school system that has one. The only difference will be the speed of processing. Even then, hand processing will often result in more rapid data return than machine processing (because of time demands usually placed on data processing equipment and the low priority instructional activities are generally accorded). Consequently, the absence of a computer cannot be used to justify a school system's failure to design an effective instructional diagnostic system or to implement sophisticated student diagnosis.

Conduct of the Pilot Test. Diagnostic systems require experimentation and modification before they yield quality data. Pilot testing serves as an effective mechanism for refining tests to the point that the teacher can derive the information he or she needs to diagnose and to place students satisfactorily and for determining the flaws in a new diagnostic system.

In pilot test situations, test designers are most interested in assessing the reactions of the users. Both positive and negative reactions will affect the nature and extent of the revisions that will need to be applied to the final test. As such, it is vital that a sufficient sample of teachers and students are used in pilot testing in order to ascertain the location, the nature, and the frequency of criticisms leveled at criterion-referenced tests, directions, and answer sheets. Test designers must avoid making test revisions based on low frequency criticisms that would not materially increase the diagnostic effectiveness of the test or would lessen that effectiveness.

Among the many features of criterion-referenced tests that will receive practitioner scrutiny during pilot testing are the following: (1) duration of administration; (2) validity of items; (3) item wording; (4) typing and printing; (5) directions to teacher or student; (6)

answer sheets; (7) selection of items; (8) sequence of items; (9) number of items for each skill; (10) information reported; (11) appropriateness of items for skills; and (12) grade level and skill span.

Special attention should be given to those test features that receive severe criticism from teachers. Inasmuch as the purpose of test design is to increase the diagnostic capabilities of teachers and obtain accurate data about students, any test characteristics frequently perceived to be problems by teachers are real flaws that test designers must explain or modify. Otherwise, teachers will have little confidence in or utility for the results garnered from the diagnostic system.

Completion of Final Test Revision. The revision of basic criterion-referenced tests into final form is a detailed process. Rarely do the final forms resemble the basic test designs because pilot testing generally exposes numerous content and procedural flaws that must be corrected if the users are to be satisfied with and committed to the final product. Consequently, it is desirable for test designers to enlist the assistance of a group of teachers to review the criticisms leveled at the basic test forms and rate the seriousness of test weaknesses. If it is possible, the review team should include a substantial portion of actual test users.

The first issue of concern will be test item validity. Each item tested should be examined on the basis of the number of correct and incorrect responses it received and the perceived level of item difficulty for students responding to it. Those items considered to be simple that have a high incidence of error should be discarded or rewritten. Responses to items for more difficult skills—generally those that would be answered correctly only by an advanced student and that many other students have answered incorrectly—must be studied with greater care and, perhaps, administered to higher level students before a judgment is made that they are not good items. Test review teams will also want to note similarities in the characteristics of students who respond incorrectly to certain test items to insure that there are not unintended, undetected biases that would cause a certain class of students to demonstrate skill deficiency when it did not exist.

Skill and item sequence is a second area of study. Student responses that show consistent erratic performances (correct-incorrect-correct) may be indicative of the misplacement of skills or items in a testing sequence. In other instances, recurring errors on a particular skill or item, preceded and followed by consistent correct responses, may indicate that a skill is unnecessary for the mastery of subsequent skills and unrelated to previous skills. In this instance, the skill and items may be extracted from the curricular program or re-located in it. Such decisions should be made, however, only after it is determined that the cause for incorrect response is not item invalidity.

The wording, selection, and appropriateness of test items will all need extensive examination in the light of analyses of students' test results and user criticisms. Each of these factors influences item validity, and attending to slight content and procedural inconsisten-cies or flaws can result in vastly improved diagnostic capacity on tests. On numerous occasions, the choice of alternate words, the selection of different illustrations or items, or the inclusion of items that are more appropriate to a select clientele or geographical area will aid in garnering more accurate diagnostic and placement data. Special care must be taken in item adjustments to insure that the goal of such activities is to increase accuracy of skill measurement and not to simplify items in an effort to improve test scores. The former is accomplished by improving item design and enhancing user understanding, while the latter is accomplished by reducing item complexity to a point where the skill in question is no longer being fairly represented. The former provides increased diagnostic accuracy; the latter yields higher yet deceptively inaccurate and unusable test scores.

Directions, answer sheets, typing and printing, and the type of information reported on the tests are concerns that may be treated together because they reflect inadequacies in the organization or presentation of the test or data. Elimination of these weaknesses is easily accomplished because they tend to center on providing more sample information, illustrations, and examples; clarifying mean-ing; using simpler vocabulary; improving production quality; rear-ranging format; and providing more or less data. Though these are nagging, real concerns, they do not present serious problems for completing final test forms.

The grade level or skill span of tests, the number of tests for each skill, and the duration of test administration are interdependent issues and must be examined simultaneously. Generally speaking, the test's grade level or skill span should be determined prior to the time that the number of items for each skill and the duration of administration are set. Test designers and teachers will seek a test with a skill span that can diagnose and aid in placing the majority of the students entering a grade level. Such a test span should be administered in a reasonable time period and insure that most students will be quickly placed to begin instruction; other students will require further testing and can then be allocated the necessary time for more detailed and probing diagnosis. Once the skill span of a test is determined (usually prior to pilot testing) only serious criticism should cause its alteration.

The number of items selected for each skill will be dependent upon the degree of confidence teachers want in diagnosing students. If the diagnostic data collected in pilot testing are frequently inconclusive in pinpointing placement, more items for each skill will need to be added. If the data gathered in testing are highly conclusive and the time taken in test administration is too great, consideration may be given to reducing the number of items representing each skill. It must be remembered, however, if reducing the number of test items measuring skills ever adversely affects the conclusiveness of diagnostic and placement data, adjustments should be made in the time taken in test administration rather than tampering with the number of items representing each skill.

Criticism of the administration time of tests is the least justifiable cause for adjusting test content. Many times such adjustments cause a reduction in the diagnostic capacity and accuracy of the tests. To respond to criticisms of testing time, testing periods or days may be spread in order to reduce student fatigue. Even though the duration of test administration may seem inordinately long in some instances, data users will recognize that initially correct diagnosis and placement will result in enormous student and teacher time savings that would be lost if tests of short duration, reduced skill span, and limited item representation were used and diagnostic data proved to be inconclusive, misleading, or inaccurate.

Conduct of Student Diagnosis. The completion of revisions on criterion-referenced tests prepares school systems for the conduct of sophisticated student diagnosis. With the administration of these tests, teachers can ascertain skill strengths and weaknesses of individual students, and these performance indicators can be used to affix instructional placement or to establish a rationale for further testing to locate final placement.

The development of instructional foundations and the creation of criterion-referenced tests insure administrators and teachers that student learning problems can be identified early and instructional placement will be effected with greater accuracy than is commonly attained in school systems that do not have these tools or are not inclined to develop them. With successful diagnostic procedures in operation in a school system, the probability of successful placement as a third step in criterion-referenced diagnosis, placement, and instruction is greatly increased.

Design Work for the Teacher

Where school systems have undertaken little diagnostic test development or selection, teachers can fill this void by completing such activities themselves. The program foundation and page number locations of those skills, concepts, and processes developed earlier provide a solid basis for beginning. These should be augmented by the same materials created for the course or grade level that precedes the one in which a diagnostic test will be designed (hopefully, this work will have been completed by one of your teacher colleagues).

For purposes of illustration, suppose it is your intention to produce a diagnostic (criterion-referenced) test for students entering sixth grade reading. (*Remember that the identical principles applied to designing a sixth grade reading test are pertinent to every other course or grade level test developed for the school system's programs.*) Beginning with the instructional program foundations that were produced earlier, you will want to prescribe a grade level span for the test. In this instance, a test that is one grade level in length is sufficient because it confines your test to a limited range of skills, concepts, and processes. Given this single grade level constraint, the skills comprising the test will include items representing the last half of the skills normally taught in fifth grade reading and the first half of the reading skills normally taught in sixth grade. Most students just entering sixth grade will be able to respond correctly to some test items, and thus, a usable test profile will be provided on each student. This is an important test characteristic. Imagine administering twenty-five sixth grade students a reading test that contained only sixth grade skills, which they have *not been* formally taught. It is conceivable that all or nearly all of the students would perform every item incorrectly. What has been learned about these students' actual learning strengths, weaknesses, and placements? Nothing.

Using the listings of skills for grades five and six reading, mark those that will be included in the test and separate them from those that will not be included. Discard the latter skills for the moment. Assume there are sixty skills (thirty from grade five and thirty from grade six) with which you are working. Examine each skill in its textual content and select, circle, or write down five test items for each skill. This number will provide you with an ample supply of items for both the basic test and a backup pool in the event that you want a broader test than you originally visualized.

In the process of selecting, circling, or writing down your test items for each skill, proceed according to the sequence of skills you developed—from the first to the last skill that will be contained in the test. Later, when you are diagnosing your students, the sequencing will have a direct bearing on how placement for instruction is determined.

Test item selection or development is not carried out without having a number of rules in mind. First, be careful that the reading difficulty of test items is the same as a fifth or sixth grade student would normally be expected to handle. This problem can be avoided by examining textbooks, workbooks, and teacher editions written for fifth and sixth grade levels when selecting test items. Normally, publishers will carefully control their text's reading levels. Second, use terminology familiar to the students and avoid jargon. Third, avoid test item directions or procedures that are likely to cause students to be confused about desired responses or to misinterpret how and where to place their answers. Fourth, if test items are taken directly from the textual, workbook, or teacher editions, modify them slightly so that later, if you decide to use the test as an end of the year evaluation instrument, you are not testing with items that are *identical* to content that was taught. If you do not modify test items and use the test for final course evaluation, you may well be accused of teaching for or to your test, which you are. By altering the items slightly, you will avoid such criticism later and be evaluating with a fair instrument. Fifth, select or develop items according to any format you like—fill-in-the-blank, multiple choice, matching, descriptive. However, avoid test items where there is a high probability that students can guess items correctly without actually knowing the correct answer (true and false items or multiple choice questions with only three choices from which the students will choose). These types of questions are poor at discerning whether or not students actually have mastered skills, concepts, or processes, and placement may be highly inaccurate if such items are used with any frequency. Sixth, remember that the purpose of diagnostic tests is to determine *fairly* which skills students can and cannot perform. Thus, select test items that represent the skill content to be taught. Do not select the most difficult or simplest items from available content but, rather, identify items of a moderate level of difficulty. Do not try to prove that your students can do well or poorly on the test you construct. You are merely the unbiased observer, and your interests must be with a fair assessment that will aid accurate placement, instruction, and increased student learning as a result of your diagnostic efforts.

Having identified five test items for each of the sixty skills, in sequence, you now have 300 test items that can be used to diagnose students entering sixth grade reading. The entire process to this point will have taken about ten to fifteen hours or so if you have had past experience with the textual materials, and the program foundations and page references were previously specified. Again, it is beneficial if you have the assistance of a few of your colleagues in these endeavors. Surely the development time will be reduced as a result of additional assistance.

At this point, it would be helpful to type or write out the skills, the page number references, and (in sequence) the test items developed. In addition, code each of the skills and items using a numbering system like the one described at the end of the chapter or one as simple as the following: (1) code the skills, concepts, and processes as Skill A, Skill B, Skill C, Skill D, and so forth, and (2) code the test items related to Skill A as A-1, A-2, A-3, A-4 and the items related to Skill B as B-1, B-2, B-3. A sample of your typewritten product may look like this:

Skill A: Comprehension of Story Meaning   HRW pp. 128–140
HM   pp. 78–84

A-1:   Circle the answer that best describes John's feelings about Mary
       in the story, "John and Mary."
A-2:   ......
A-3:   ......
Skill B: Fantasy and Fact   HRW pp. 141–147
                              HM   pp. 62–68
B-1:   Select the ending that you believe could really have happened.
B-2:   ......
B-3:   ......

The next step in test design is referencing the sixty skills to one
another. This is an activity that can be delayed until you are more
familiar with the relationship of various skills, an awareness that
comes with increased usage of diagnostic tests in testing students
and familiarity with the layout and design of your textbooks and
materials. In the event that such experiences are already well developed, skill cross-referencing is very simple. It merely involves
listing alongside each skill the codes for other earlier skills that
should have been mastered before the student undertakes mastering the latest skill. Thus, if students should have been exposed to or
mastered Skill A before undertaking Skill B, then Skill A will be
listed alongside of Skill B as a reminder of its prerequisite importance to students as they begin instruction on Skill B. This citation
may be done in the following manner:

Skill B: Fantasy and Fact   HRW pp. 141–147
   (A)   HM   pp. 62–68

This referencing is carried out for each of the sixty skills. Some of
the skills may have multiple cross-references; others may have relatively few.
    Prior to the organization of the test into a pilot form, it may be
valuable to review the activities undertaken to this point: (1) skills,
concepts, and processes were identified and listed for grades 5 and 6;
(2) a span for the test was set at one grade level—from the midpoint
of grade five reading skills to the midpoint of grade six reading
skills; (3) sixty skills were selected in that grade range around
which five test items for each skill would be identified or developed;
(4) proceeding in sequence from the first to the sixtieth skill, five
test items were selected (and modified) from textual materials or
developed for each of the sixty skills; (5) these items were selected to

serve as a part of both the basic test and as a residual item pool; (6) the skills and test items were referenced to textbook and material content; (7) the skills and test items were coded; (8) the test items appropriate to a given skill were referenced to that skill; and (9) each skill was cross-referenced to other dependent skills. All of this information has been typed or written in the specific sequence that the skills will normally be taught to students.

A determination will now need to be made on the duration of test administration and, consequently, the number of items that will represent each skill on the test form. Because sixth grade students are to be tested, assume that a decision is made to test over a three-day span and use three items to represent each skill. The test form then will contain 180 items, perhaps divided in three sections that can be used on successive days.

You are ready to construct the basic test. Begin by making a few photocopies of your typewritten skills and items. Using one copy, take the five items that represent your first skill, cut them apart, turn them face down, mix, and select three random items to represent the skill in the basic test. Tape these items onto a blank sheet of paper and repeat the same procedure for the second skill, the third one, and so on. Remember to select your test items for skills in the exact sequence that the skills appeared on your original listing (or according to the sequence in which the skills will be taught in class). Mark on one of the remaining complete copies of your skills and items those items that are contained in the basic test and those items that are currently a part of the test item pool.

Organize the basic test and retype it in a fashion similar to any of the sample tests provided at the end of this chapter. More than likely, in a trial test run, test directions will be contained in the test items and special answer sheets will be unnecessary, as answers will be placed directly on to the test form. Thus, no further elaboration need be made on these matters.

You are now ready to administer the pilot test to your students. Carry out the test as you would any other one, but reserve more than ample time for testing so that all students will complete every item they possibly can. Criterion-referenced diagnostic tests are not power or speed tests. They are designed to ascertain what students can perform under relaxed conditions.

After administering and correcting the tests, develop a grid or matrix (see figure 4) and insert the students' name, the skills tested, and each student's test results on each skill. Note correct responses to a test item with a +, incorrect responses with a −, and blanks where students have not responded to test items. This information will be used to examine points in your test where items appear to be invalid, program gaps occur, articulation problems may exist, skills may be out of sequence, or any number of other problems. On the basis of information acquired from pilot testing, examine the con-

Fig. 4
Diagnostic Grid

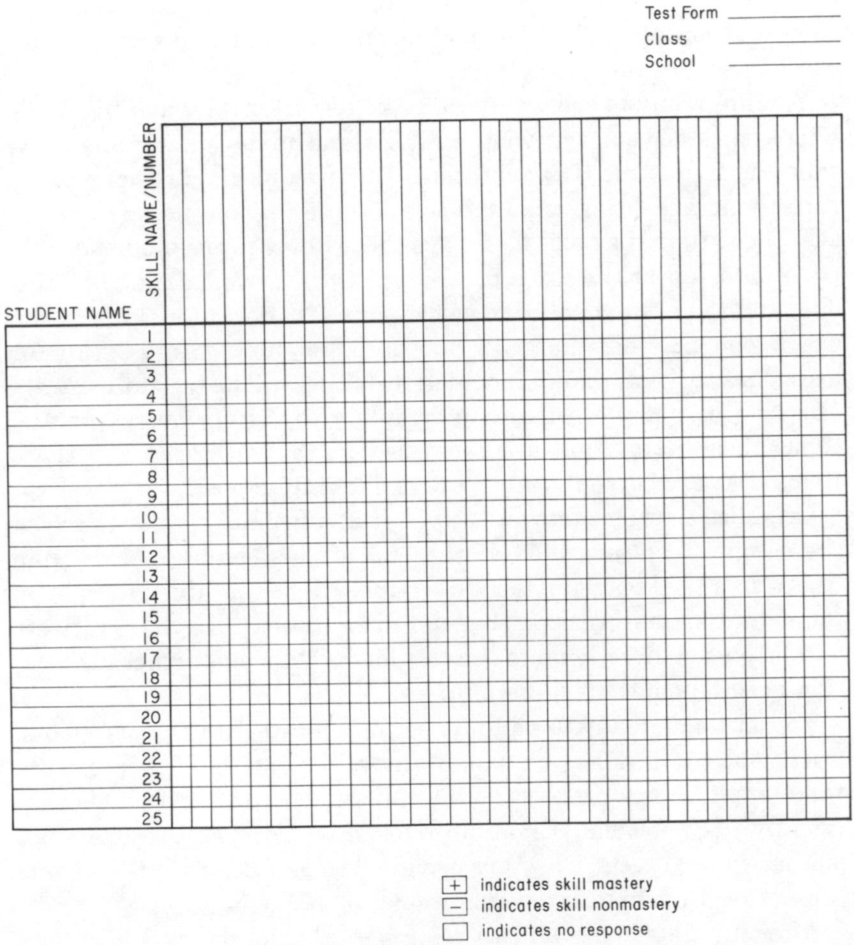

+ indicates skill mastery
− indicates skill nonmastery
☐ indicates no response

tent detailed earlier in this chapter and the information provided in chapter 4 to organize your final test form. Basically, in final test construction, you will want to make sure that test alterations are made on the basis of a high frequency of incorrect responses by students that cannot be resolved by simple explanations (for example, none of the students have been exposed to that skill) but, rather, illustrate erratic performance, confusion, difficulty in interpretation, or other factors related to poor program, item, sequence, wording, design, direction, or answer characteristics or specifications. These latter characteristics are the ones to which you will want to attend first.

Locally developed tests become more and more refined with usage and the application of information gathered in subsequent testings. Even the most sophisticated commercial testing firms learn about their design mistakes through trial and error. Thus, there is every reason to be confident that painstaking test development and monitoring of testing results by classroom teachers and school systems can lead to the creation of test forms that will yield valid and reliable diagnostic information. With careful development, these tests can dramatically improve the teacher's accuracy in placing and instructing students. In time, these efforts will result in measurably improved achievement gains for students and greater teacher confidence in carrying out instructional programs.

Documents

Document 3 is a numbering system that may be used to code skills, test items, and later instructional units for the purposes of referencing, cross-referencing, organizing, and filing.

Document 4 is a single skill criterion-referenced test that may be developed by teachers to preassess or postassess a student's readiness for or acquisition of a single instructional skill. These single skill criterion-referenced tests (often called pretests and posttests) are fine tools for the classroom teacher to use in daily instruction. They do have, however, limited utility for classroom diagnosis and placement because of their focus on a single skill.

Multiple skill criterion-referenced tests, as exemplified by document 5, are instruments used to diagnose skill strengths and weaknesses, determine student placement, or ascertain retention of previously mastered skills. The skill range of a multiple skill criterion-referenced test is generally only four to eight skills. Consequently, it is not a sound grade level diagnostic and placement instrument. Nonetheless, coupling several of these tests together can furnish an effective single or multigrade level diagnostic and placement instrument. Multiple skill criterion-referenced tests are particularly effective for checking student retention over a broader skill span than the single skill criterion-referenced test.

Document 6 is a sixth grade level criterion-referenced test used to determine students' beginning skill strengths, weaknesses, and placements at the beginning of a school year. Its skill span is sufficient to insure the effective diagnosis and placement of the majority of students in a given classroom with reliable accuracy. In addition, other lower or higher grade level criterion-referenced tests may be used in conjunction with the first test to strengthen diagnosis. In this instance, students' strengths, weaknesses, and placement positions can be broadly ascertained over a range of grade levels or courses. Appropriate multiple skill criterion-referenced tests (which have more items representing each skill than do the grade level tests) could be administered as a backup to reaffirm the accuracy of the original diagnosis and placement using the grade level criterion-referenced tests if such thoroughness is desired.

Document 3
Numbering System for Skills, Test Items, and Instructional Units

A numbering system aids teachers to identify quickly the (1) subject, (2) grade level, (3) location in sequence, and (4) purpose or function of the page or section of an instructional unit (this latter characteristic applies mainly to instructional units developed by teachers, as in chapter 5) of a given skill, test item, or instructional unit. Further, it has substantial value for referencing, cross-referencing, organizing, filing, locating, and reproducing original source documents and previously developed materials.

The numbering system works by merely picking appropriate letters and numbers from the tables below that coincide with the subject, grade level, location in sequence, and purpose or function of whatever is being coded.

Let us suppose the first skill in a sixth grade reading program foundation were to be coded. Examining the tables below, the subject, reading, is coded first.

RD

Next, the grade level—sixth in this case—is selected.

401–

Third, the sequence of the skill in the program foundation (for that grade level) is coded. In this case, the first skill is being considered.

005

Finally, because a skill from the program foundation is being coded, the format number is always selected.

.00

Thus, the completed coding of the first skill in a sixth grade reading program foundation is:

RD 401–005.00

The next skills in the sixth grade reading program foundation would be coded as:

RD 401–010.00
RD 401–015.00
RD 401–020.00

Any other skills, items, and instructional units to be coded are done so by repeating the procedure previously specified. Namely, determine the subject, the grade level where the skill is taught, the skill's location in sequence, and purpose or function of the page or section, search the tables below, and write the code in sequenced order.

A. Subject Codes (limited sample):

RD	Reading K–12	SO	Social Studies K–9
MA	Mathematics K–9	PE	Physical Education K–12
LA	Language Arts K–6	MU	Music K–6
SG	Spelling K–6	SE	Special Education—Educable
HW	Handwriting K–6	ST	Special Education—Trainable
AR	Art K–12	LS	Life Science
SC	Science K–6	ES	Earth Science
PS	Physical Science	FR	French
LI	Literature	SP	Spanish
EN	English	LT	Latin
TY	Typing	GE	German
HE	Home Economics	SH	Shorthand

AM	Auto Mechanics	AC	Accounting
CH	Chemistry	AL	Algebra
PH	Physics	GT	Geometry
BI	Biology	TR	Trigonometry
Im	Instrumental Music	CA	Calculus
GM	General Music	BK	Bookkeeping
SS	Strings	WO	Woods
		ME	Metals
		DR	Drafting
		WH	World History
		WP	World Problems
		AS	American Studies

B. Grade Level Codes:

101	Kindergarten	451	Seventh Grade
151	First Grade	501	Eighth Grade
201	Second Grade	551	Ninth Grade
251	Third Grade	601	Tenth Grade
301	Fourth Grade	651	Eleventh Grade
351	Fifth Grade	701	Twelfth Grade
401	Sixth Grade		

C. Location (of skill or learning unit) in Sequence:

005	= 1st Position	040	= 8th Position
010	= 2nd Position	045	= 9th Position
015	= 3rd Position	050	= 10th Position
020	= 4th Position	055	= 11th Position
025	= 5th Position	060	= 12th Position
030	= 6th Position	065	= 13th Position
035	= 7th Position	070	= 14th Position

D. Purpose or Function of the Page or Section:

.00	Format page or skill sequence	.07	Third Post-test
.01	Pretest	.08	Key for Third Post-test
.02	Pretest	.09	Fourth Post-test
.03	First Post-test	.10	Key for Fourth Post-test
.04	Key for First Post-test	.11–99	Instructional experience
.05	Second Post-test		constructed for the
.06	Key for Second Post-test		package such as study
			guides, worksheets, texts,
			of lectures, and enrichment
			materials.

E. Numbering System Applications:

Two Letters	Three Numerals	Three Numerals and Two Place Decimal
Mathematics	Fourth Grade	Fiftieth Skill in Skill Sequence
MA	301	250.00

MA 301–250.00
MA = Mathematics
301 = Fourth Grade
250 = 50th Skill
.00 = Skill Sequence

ES 451–095.00
ES = Earth Science
451 = Seventh Grade
095 = 19th Skill
.00 = Skill Sequence

LI 701–120.00
LI = Literature
701 = Twelfth Grade
120 = 24th Skill
.00 = Skill Sequence

Document 4
Single Skill Criterion-Referenced Test:
Senior High School Consumer Mathematics

1. Dr. Zimmers last year put aside $279 toward a summer trip abroad that he has been planning with some of his friends. He will need $450 for the trip. How much must he budget for this during each of the next six months before the trip? How much will this leave from his monthly income from part-time work of $125?

2. Mr. River's mortgage payment is $125.00 a month. This includes taxes and insurance. He has spent an average of $150 a year for maintenance, and the average cost of all utilities is $35 a month. What percent of Mr. River's salary of $9000 a year should he budget for housing?

3. Tim expects to work full time, 37 hours a week, during 10 weeks next year when school is not in session. How much will Tim's take-home pay be for 10 weeks if he is paid $2.20 an hour and 15% of this is withheld?

4. Mr. Kee estimates that it costs about 13¢ a mile to drive his car and that he will drive it about 13,000 miles next year. What will his automobile expenses be for the year?

5. A sample budget for a low income allows 32% for housing. If the low income budgeted is $5000 a year after deductions, how much of this is assumed to be spent for housing?

6. The Tallmen's budgeted $2100 for housing. How much more or less is this than 25% of their income if their income is $7000?

Document 5
Multiple Skill Criterion-Referenced Test:
Eighth Grade Reading

(12 out of 14)

I.

1. The snapper lay large and dark green in the headlight beams. It moved a little and left razorlike claw marks in the wet sand.

   What does this paragraph describe? _____

2. Bill's face was serious as he raised his instrument. He placed it under his chin and stroked the bow across the strings. The music began.

   What instrument do you picture? _____

3. She traveled through the night as though nothing would harm her. She was strong.

   What do you think *she* is? _____
   Her sleek body and wings slid into the sky as her motor roared.

   Given these extra details, what is *her* real identity? _____

II. In the sentences below underline each example of figurative language.

1. A nine-year-old tornado had ripped through the bedroom scattering socks, pillows, gym shoes, and underwear in his wake.

2. The clouds were like ribbons flung across the sky.

3. During his illness, Steve was as pale as a ghost.

III. Match each item of punctuation in column A with the description of the oral interpretation of it in column B by writing the correct letter in the blank to the left of the number.

Column A	Column B
____1. comma (,)	a—voice should show excitement
____2. dash (—)	b—a short pause
____3. exclamation mark (!)	c—an abrupt break in thought, a short pause is necessary

Read each selection and circle the letter of the word that best describes the vocal expression that it should be given when read aloud.

4. Beside ourselves
   (It is for us they run!)

We shout and pound the stands:
For one to win.

    a. seriousness   b. excitement   c. sorrow

5. Now the dark waters at the bow fold back, like earth against the plow, foam brightens like the dogwood now at home, in my own country.

    a. joy   b. happiness   c. longing

IV.
1. Circle the letter of the word that best describes the author's tone in this selection.

    I don't see how she could have become a cheerleader. I've had much more training and experience than she has. Besides she's nothing but a teacher's pet.

    a. happy   b. jealous   c. sad   d. excited

2. Circle the letter of the word that best describes the mood of this selection.

    The stands shook as the crowd jumped with excitement over the victory. Their voices rose to screams, which shrilled through the night air.

    a. bitter   b. enthusiastic   c. sad   d. angry

3. Circle the letter of the word that best describes the mood of this selection.
    The news of the car accident came as a great blow to me. How could he die? He was so young and just beginning a successful career. This is what a tragedy truly is.

    a. upset   b. frightened   c. envious   d. distrustful

Document 6
Manual of Directions:
Sixth Level Reading Placement Tests, Levels 5½ to 6½

General Instructions for Teachers
(4–6)

1. Before beginning the test, the teacher should see that each student has a #2 lead pencil for marking answers. An extra supply of pencils should be at hand.
2. When administering the test, the teacher should have a blank copy of the test for demonstrating along with giving directions.

3. A natural classroom situation should be maintained.

4. During the testing period, the teacher should move quietly about the room to see that instructions are being followed.

5. It is important that students be prevented from helping each other in order to obtain a true picture of each child's placement.

6. The teacher is to read the instructions that are underscored to the students. If you find it necessary to deviate from the underscored instructions, please send us a note indicating the question number and changes made.

7. Answer sheets are to be used. No marks should be made in the test booklet. The teacher may choose to enter and grid the test ID information below the name grid on the answer sheet before test administration. A list of school codes is provided at the back of this manual for your reference. For all levels the form of the test is A. The grade coded should be the grade level indicated for the placement test administered. Each student's birthdate should be coded in numeral form.

8. This placement test may be given in one sitting. It is estimated that the test will take between 30 and 45 minutes.

9. Before returning the answer sheets to the office for scoring, the teacher should check all forms for the following:

A) Was a #2 lead pencil used?

B) Did each student grid his name properly, including middle initial?

C) Are the teacher's initials properly coded?

D) Is school code, grade, birthdate and form of test gridded properly?

E) Are question responses marked properly?

The teacher should correct any errors occurring in the name and test ID area. Be sure to complete the cover sheet and indicate the total number of students tested.

Specific Directions for Administering

NOTES

(1) The terminology used in this test is consistent with the adopted text. However, feel free to use any vocabulary with which your children are familiar. It is suggested that you read through the directions prior to administering the tests and make any terminology changes you feel are necessary.

(2) If it is apparent that the children have reached their frustration level, discontinue testing because the placement position will have been already determined.

(3) Each level of the placement tests covers approximately a one year span

from one-half year below grade level to one-half year above grade level. Most of the students in the district should fall within this range. However, for students who are exceptionally bright or exceptionally slow higher or lower level forms of the reading placement test should be administered.

Teacher to pupils, SAY:

> *You are going to take a reading test. I will give each of you an answer sheet on which you are to mark* ALL *of your answers. Don't make any marks on it until you are told to do so.*

Distribute the answer sheets, SAY:

> *Turn your answer sheet sideways so that the name grid is on your right.* [Demonstrate] *Look at the lines on the left that are provided for your name, school, instructor, grade and test. Print your last name first, then your first name.* [Pause] *I have put the test form on the board* [take from the cover of the manual or test booklet]. *Now fill in the rest of the information in the space provided* [hold up answer sheet and demonstrate]. *Be sure to print.*

See that all students have the right place and give help with teacher's name, etc., as needed. After all descriptive information has been entered, SAY:

> *Now look at the name grid on the right. Print my initials* [put them on the board] *in the first three boxes under "class." Use one box for each letter. In the column below each box, fill in the space that has the same letter as the letter in the box.*
> *Now, print your last name first, and then print your first name and middle initial in the boxes provided for them. Use one box for each letter. If any part of your last name or your first name is too long to fit into the spaces provided, print as many letters as you can, but do not let your last name run into the boxes provided for your first name.* [Pause] *Now in the column below each box, fill in the space that has the same letter as the letter in the box. Be sure that there is one and only one space marked in each column. Fill in the blank space at the top of every column in which you have* NOT *marked a letter. Be sure to make heavy, shiny marks that cover the whole space. If you make a mistake, erase it carefully. If you have any questions, raise your hand.*

Pause until all students have finished filling in the name grid. Give individual help as needed. Then, SAY:

You should have exactly twenty-three spaces marked on your grid including my initials and your name. Count to make sure.

After the students have checked their name grids, SAY: (Note: If you have previously completed this section of the grid, skip to the directions for the sample items.)

Now look at the grid below where you printed your name. [Demonstrate] *The first three columns say school. I will put our school code on the board.* [A list of school codes has been provided at the back of this manual for your reference.] *Use one box for each number. In the column below each box, fill in the space that has the same number as the number in the box.* [Pause] *The next column is grade.* [For grade, use the level of the placement exam being administered.] *Write the grade level in the box and mark the space below it that has the same number.* [Pause] *Now look at the columns that say birthdate. Write your birthdate in numeral form in the boxes at the top. For example: If you were born on July 8, 1974 you would write 07/08/64, because July is the seventh month. If you have any questions about how to write your birthdate, raise your hand and I will help you. Remember there must be a number in every box.* [Pause and give help as needed.] *Now in the column under each box fill in the space that has the same number as the number in the box.* [Pause] *In the last column which says "form of this test is" write the letter A in the box and mark the space that says A.* [Pause] *You should have exactly 11 marks in this section of the grid. Count them to make sure.*

To start administer the test SAY:

I am going to tell you how to use your answer sheet. Listen carefully so that you will know how to mark your answers properly. You are to mark all of your answers on your answer sheet. Do not make any marks in your test booklet. For each question, choose the best answer. Then, on your answer sheet, find the item number for the question. Mark the space for your answer. Be sure each mark is heavy and shiny and fills the answer space. If you make a mistake, erase the wrong mark completely. Do not make any stray marks on your answer sheet. Are there any questions?

Point to the sample questions, then SAY:

Now look at sample item A. Find the word among the three choices that stands for the contraction of "I would." [Pause] *The correct answer is "I'd" which is above the letter c. Now on your answer sheet, find sample item A.* [Point] *Fill in the space above "c" on your answer sheet.*

Now look at sample item B. Find the word among the three choices that does not have the ō sound. [Pause] *The correct answer is "bond" which is above the letter b. Now on your answer sheet, find sample item B.* [Point] *Fill in the space above "b" on your answer sheet.*

You will mark all of your answers like these two sample items.

Open your test booklet. You will have to read the question and choose the best answer. If you are not sure of the answer to a question, make the best choice you can but do not make wild guesses. Remember, mark all of your answers on your answer sheet and MARK ONLY ONE ANSWER FOR EACH QUESTION.

Once you have finished a page, do not turn back in your test booklet. Turn your book over on your desk when you have finished this test.

NOTE TO TEACHER: REFER TO TEST BOOKLET FOR QUESTIONS.

SIXTH YEAR READING PLACEMENT, LEVELS 5½ TO 6½

Sample Items

A.

I'll	I'm	I'd
a	*b*	*c*

B.

boat	bond	bone
a	*b*	*c*

1. The underlined vowel sound in to͜uch, cu͟p, and bu͟lky are pronounced with the symbol of:

    a. u   b. u̇   c. i   d. ô

2. The underlined vowel sound in la͟unch, bro͟ad, and co͟ugh are pronounced with the symbol of:

    a. ə   b. ô   c. e   d. a

3. The underlined vowel sound bu͟sh, go͟od, and fu͟ll are pronounced with the symbol of:

    a. u   b. ô   c. u̇   d. ō

4. The underlined vowel sound in be<u>e</u>n, b<u>ui</u>ld, and p<u>i</u>n are pronounced with the symbol of:

    a. e   b. i   c. ə   d. ĭ

5. The underlined vowel sound in lunch<u>eo</u>n, miss<u>io</u>n, and tak<u>e</u>n are pronounced with the symbol of:

    a. u̇   b. ə   c. i   d. ô

6. The first syllable in dedicate is accented. When "ion" is added, the accent mark is on syllable:

    a. four   b. two   c. three   d. one

7. In which word do you hear the (a) sound?

    a. back   b. crown   c. straight   d. rate

8. In which word do you hear the (ô) sound?

    a. April   b. music   c. faucet   d. rope

9. In which word do you hear the (ĭ) sound?

    a. antique   b. turnip   c. amaze   d. guide

10. Which letter or letters spell the (ch) sound in adventure?

    a. tu   b. t   c. nt   d. d

11. What word contains the /ā/ sound?

    a. age   b. care   c. hat   d. dare

12. Which word has the primary and secondary stress marked correctly?

    a. cul′ti vat′ed   c. cul ti vat′ed′
    b. cul′ti′vat ed   d. cul′ti vat ed′

13. What is the other phonetic spelling of the given word?
    bow (bō)?
    a. bou   b. bōl   c. bē   d. bo

14. Which word has a short vowel sound in the accented syllable?

    a. music   b. public   c. grateful   d. promote

15. Which example shows the correct marking of the word part receiving primary stress?

    a. <u>dis</u>graceful   b. disgrace<u>ful</u>   c. dis<u>graceful</u>   d. none of these

16. Which word has a different stress pattern from the other compound words?

    a. sightseer   b. uphold   c. honeycomb   d. housekeeper

17. Which vowel-consonant pattern is correct?

    po/et/ic

    a. cv/vv/vc
    b. cc/vc/vc
    c. cv/vc/vc
    d. cv/cv/cv

18. Which word (or words) completes this sentence?
    The _____ were blooming early.

    a. two lips   b. tulips   c. tulops   d. toulips

19. Which word has the primary stress marked correctly?

    a. <u>hur</u>ricane   b. hurri<u>cane</u>   c. hur<u>ri</u>cane   d. none of these

20. Which word shows correct stress placement?

    a. <u>sus</u>picious   b. sus<u>pi</u>cious   c. suspi<u>cious</u>   d. none of these

21. Which word *does not* have the same consonant sound as the others?

    a. late   b. sentence   c. migration   d. writing

22. The prefix "un" may be used with all but one of the following endings. Which ending is that?

    a. able   b. spire   c. like   d. armed

23. What is the underlined part of "<u>in</u>doors"?

    a. root   b. base   c. an affix   d. suffix

24. Complete the following sentence.
    A hospital is a _____ organization.

    a. profit   b. nonprofit   c. reprofit   d. antiprofit

25. Complete the following sentence.
    Antibodies in the blood help _____ the spread of germs and infection.

    a. act   b. counteract   c. react   d. overact

26. Which word best completes the sentence?
    The mirror _____ his image.

    a. inflected   b. reflected   c. insisted   d. resisted

27. Which prefix would you use to complete the following sentence?
    His story _____scends belief.

    a. tran   b. ad   c. circum   d. re

28. Which word completes the sentence?

    A figure with three sides is a _____.
    a. rectangle   b. triangle   c. square   d. circle

29. Which word best completes the following sentence?
    A rainbow has many colors; it is _____.

    a. multifeatured   c. multicolored
    b. microscopic   d. tincolored

30. What is the meaning for the Greek prefix *homo* as in homogeneous?

    a. same, like   c. not
    b. against   d. with

31. Which prefix below would you use to complete this sentence?
    There will be a ten-minute _____mission between the first two acts
    of the play.

    a. extra   b. intra   c. inter   d. anti

32. What describes the underlined word?
    The simplest kind of camera is far from being a complex mechanism.

    a. simple   c. complicated
    b. comfortable   d. perforated

33. Which word below is an antonym for "began"?
    When Karen was given the lead in the school play, she got carried
    away and began acting her part even when she was offstage.

    a. started   b. finished   c. completed   d. continued

34. Using the context as a clue, what is the best meaning for the under-lined word?

    "Look at these <u>antiquated</u> books," said Linda. "This one was published way back in 1904."

    a. dusty   b. very old   c. recent   d. unused

35.   The people themselves have little, but they have found contentment by the sea, with its islands on the horizon and behind them, the mountain to which their homes are anchored.

    Think of the meaning of the word little in the above sentence. Which sentence below has that same word used with the same meaning?

    a. Have a *little* of this cake.
    b. Sit a *little* with me.
    c. He knew *little* what lay ahead.
    d. He was a *little* man.

36. Your muscles contract when you bend your elbow.
    Which word is an antonym of the word *contract* in the sentence above?

    a. blend   b. support   c. expand   d. lessen

37. Which sentence shows suspense?

    a. As the pilot throttled the big jet into the air, suddenly there was a loud pop and the engine stalled.
    b. Don't strain your eyes by reading in the dark.
    c. He lifted his rifle to his shoulder.
    d. Who won the basketball game?

38. Identify the following sentence as to person.
    They sang the anthem so beautifully the audience was spellbound.

    a. 1st   b. 2nd   c. 3rd   d. 4th

39. John dashed like a streak.
    This sentence contains a

    a. simile   b. metaphor   c. homophone   d. synonym

READ:

It is difficult to imagine the miserable and unsanitary conditions of our larger cities just a century ago. The streets were narrow and unpaved. They had no drainage system, and mud and dirt would collect after every rain. Besides, garbage and other refuse were ordinarily thrown into the street. Sewage was allowed to soak down into the earth. As a result, disease germs in the waste from human bodies would gradually drain down into the wells from which people obtained their drinking water.

Today we have tried to improve the sanitary conditions in our large cities. We have paved streets which are swept and kept clean by city crews. There are sewers to help drain off excess water. Garbage is picked up from homes and cities at least once a week by city-hired men. We have water purification systems to keep our drinking water pure and free from germs.

40. Which is the best contrast for the given statement?
    Cities a century ago had no drainage system.

    a. Cities today have paved streets.
    b. Cities today have garbage picked up.
    c. Cities today have sewer systems.
    d. Cities today have water purification systems.

41. Which statement best describes the theme of the paragraphs above?

    a. The improvements of today's cities.
    b. Sanitary conditions of cities today and cities one hundred years ago.
    c. The poisoned water of olden cities.
    d. Drinking water must be pure and free from germs.

42. Which sentence is an example of personification?

    a. He could still see the yawning mouth of the volcano.
    b. The volcano spilled lava over the island.
    c. They saw the burning pit of the volcano.
    d. Mary ran from the volcano.

43. Which paragraph contains factual evidence?

    a. Plants make up part of the land's living things. They also make up part of the living things in the sea. The most important plants of the sea are microscopic in size.
    b. The family had followed Jiya, and now they stood about him. Kino did not know what to say, for his heart ached for his friend-brother. Kino's mother was wiping her eyes, and even little Setsu looked sad. But Jiya could not speak. He kept on looking at the ocean.
    c. Both paragraphs.
    d. Neither paragraph.

READ:

The first day's climb was easy. The seven mountaineers were full of good spirits as they made camp at 11,000 feet. They laughed and sang till long after dusk, and at the first light of day were on the way again.

By 10:00 A.M. the climbers were at 14,000 feet. They had only a few more hundred upward feet to go. But from this point the east face was an almost upright wall, impossible to climb. For a little while they followed the crest of the northwest ridge. Then they saw they would have to cross over to the north face and creep up the edge of that instead.

So they crossed. To their dismay they found the North Face covered with a thin layer of ice. It would take all their mountaineering skill to climb it. With one slip, a man might fall all the way to the Matterhorn glacier, 4,000 feet below. They roped up for safety and moved forward one by one.

For about 400 feet they made their way thus across the North Face. Then they went straight up for 60 feet and cut back to the crest of the northeast ridge. Here they met another difficulty. At the very top of the ridge a rock protruded. They had somehow to get around it. Advancing with the greatest care, they made it. When they looked up, their hearts began to pound with joy, for now only an easy snow slope was above them.

The successful mountaineers remained at the top for an hour. They were so happy that they danced around wildly. Matterhorn the unconquerable had been conquered!

44. Read the above selection and decide what the mountaineers did when they came to the top of the northeast ridge and encountered a protruding rock.

   a. advanced with great care.
   b. roped up the rock.
   c. turned around and went another way.
   d. crept along the North Face.

45. According to the selection the problem of the North Face of the mountain being covered with a thin layer of ice was solved by

   a. turning around and going back.
   b. taking a chance going one by one.
   c. roping up and moving forward one by one.
   d. advancing forward with the greatest care.

46. Using the selection, find out why the mountaineers followed the crest of the northwest ridge.

   a. the east face was an almost upright wall.
   b. thin layer of ice everywhere.

    c. a rock protruded from the top of the ridge.

    d. All of the above.

47. Write the letter of the sentence that contains *both* a given fact and an explanation for that fact.

    a. The Oregon Trail and the Santa Fe Trail were two important trails in the West.

    b. With the coming of the railroad, the trails east of the Mississippi lost their importance.

    c. The Santa Fe trail went through the southwestern part of the United States.

    d. None of the above.

48. Match the cause with the effect by selecting the correct statement below.

    a. They go down to the deepest parts of the sea after dead plants and animals.

    b. They grow to a weight of 100 pounds.

    c. Some bacteria are helpful and some are not.

    d. All bacteria are small.

49. Which is the color for love?

    a. red   b. blue   c. yellow   d. white

READ:

    a. The waves lapped ever so gently over the white sand and then rolled lazily back to sea. b. On land, several sea gulls picked at the picnic leftovers beside the charred wood of a dead bonfire. c. At sea, a lone sailboat crossed the streak of moonlight and glided slowly past, barely moving in the faint breeze.

50. You will have to use the skill of inference in order to answer the question. According to the paragraph above, which phrase best completes the sentence?
The weather is _____.

    a. rainy   b. foggy   c. clear   d. snowy

51. Mark the letter in the paragraph above, that supports the following statement.

The time is late evening.

52.

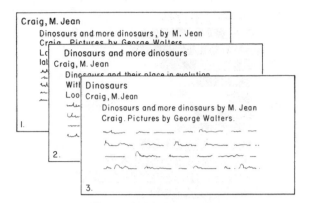

Which card of the examples given is the subject card?

a. 1   b. 2   c. 3   d. none of these

53.

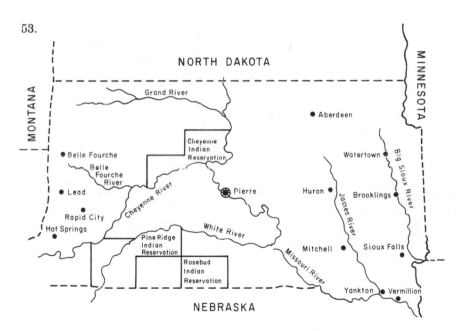

What River flows through the Pine Ridge Indian Reservation?

a. Cheyenne   b. Grand   c. White   d. Missouri

54.

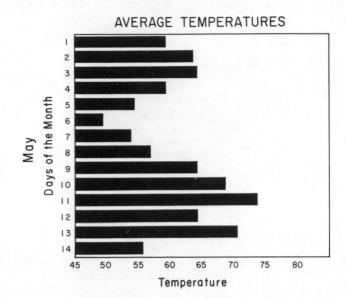

AVERAGE TEMPERATURES

Which was the warmest day?

a. May 6   b. May 11   c. May 1   d. May 13

4.   Placement

Placement is the process of identifying the point at which a student's instruction should begin in a program foundation to insure the greatest probability of future learning. It is the vital mediating process between diagnosis and instruction. Placement information pinpoints *where* diagnosed weaknesses can best be treated with techniques and materials in the school system's programs. The implication of successful placement is sound instruction characterized by qualitative and quantitative gains in student learning.

The inadequacies of diagnostic testing systems and instructional program foundations in most school systems cause student placement procedures to be relatively unrefined. Many school systems do not undertake formal and uniform diagnostic testing but rely on scanty results from standardized achievement test administration. As a consequence, teachers desiring placement data beyond those provided by standardized tests are on their own in acquiring additional, specific information on students' diagnosed skill strengths and weaknesses. They often must select, administer, correct, and interpret the results of a diagnostic test without knowledgeable assistance and, many times, in the absence of formal district sanction. Even presuming they can ably perform these activities and garner some useful diagnostic data, the problem of placing students for instruction remains. The successful accomplishment of instructional placement presumes that teachers or the school system can match or overlay student diagnostic data on the school system's instructional program foundation and locate a "best fit" or placement for each student to begin instruction. Where school systems have failed to specify program foundations, the teacher is hampered in, if not prevented from, effecting accurate placement because skill weaknesses cannot be linked back to a point of instruction. Even highly sophisticated diagnostic information is of minimal value if the teacher cannot apply it to the location of skill weaknesses in a program foundation, placement, and the delivery of instructional materials that will resolve the diagnosed learning problems.

In school systems where diagnostic testing is not a normal operational procedure and instructional program foundations do not exist or are not formalized, some form of placement is carried out anyway because students do have to be instructed. Among the more common procedures used in determining instructional placement are: (1) review of cumulative record cards, (2) review of anecdotal records, (3) examination of standardized achievement test results, (4) examination of academic grades, (5) communication with previous teachers, (6) administration of inventories, and (7) observation of the student. Information provided as a result of these procedures generally includes the degree of the student's prior success (or failure); subjective assessments of work habits; academic relationships to groups of students; indications of certain skills that were or were not successfully performed; and, in some instances, the student's last placement position. None of these data is undeniably reputable in making a determination about students' instructional placement positions.

Most often, cumulative record cards, anecdotal records, academic grades, and communications with previous teachers merely reflect a status report on how students "fit" with instructional programs in past years. If students were misplaced in programs and they performed poorly, most of the data gathered has questionable utility— it cannot be used to make any firm judgments about students except that previous placements were not correct. In these instances, judgments made on the basis of stated success in instructional programs, work habits, relationships to the group, skill strengths and weaknesses, and previous placement positions may be highly erroneous.

In a similar manner, standardized achievement tests are of limited value in placing a student. They are not designed to yield placement information. Their data merely reflect students' achievement relationships to a norm group, and though information may be gathered on a limited cluster of skills, poor performance on these tests furnishes few leads on instructional placement. Because of the narrow grade level range measured by these tests, deficient students generally do so poorly and proficient students so well on them it is questionable that the tests garner really crucial data— information that lies below or above the grade level assessed by the test. In the case of the poor students, standardized achievement tests more often than not expose the "effects" of previous skill weakness and not the basic skill deficiencies themselves. When they do uncover actual skill weaknesses, the tests provide no leads on how to remove or prevent them.

Administration of diagnostic inventories and observations of the student in instructional activities are sound procedures for determining instructional placement. In the absence of identified instructional program foundations in a school system, however, final student placement must be done without knowing how and where to connect tested and observed learning weaknesses to a textbook, workbook, or class presentation. As such, placement becomes a trial and error process. The teacher merely guesses at where the student should be placed and waits to see the outcome of instruction. If the student begins to progress after placement, there is reasonable assurance that placement was correctly performed. If the student fails, the teacher can only guess where subsequent placements should be attempted. In too many instances in the absence of identified program foundations, instructional placement is reduced to a succession of time-consuming guesses.

Trial and error placement is not uncommon in school systems. Such experimental placement procedures are employed to fill a void created by the unavailability of sound diagnostic tests that are linked to specified instructional program foundations. For many students, this type of placement does not prove to be damaging; they catch up, repeat, or compensate for misplacement in one way or another. For other students, trial and error placement is so far removed from true placement that the student is crushed by or lost in the instructional program.

Values of Correct Instructional Placement

Accurate identification of the instructional placement positions of students is a valuable aid to classroom teachers. Obviously, the closer classroom teachers approximate students' true placement positions the greater is the probability of future learning. This is the most significant derivative of establishing correct placement. Several other benefits also accrue to school systems that are placing students correctly for instruction. The following are some that have significant applications for increasing the effectiveness and efficiency of classroom teachers and the instructional success of students: (1) identification of an acquired skill base, (2) identification of skill weaknesses, (3) elimination of extraneous variables, (4) assistance in establishing instructional groups, (5) assistance in selecting appropriate instructional materials, (6) conservation of time, (7) reduction of student frustration, (8) specification of need for curricular revision, and (9) projection of need for flexible curricular program design.

Identification of an Acquired Skill Base. In the school system where program foundations have been specified and criterion-referenced tests developed, accurate placement aids the teachers in determining a student's acquired skill base. An acquired skill base is the collection of program skills that a student has previously mastered and can transfer or apply to learning slightly more difficult program skills. The acquired skill base aids the student to attack, solve, and acquire future skills. The further a student is placed from his acquired skill base and, hence, the greater the number of unmastered skills between the acquired skill base and placement, the more improbable it is that he will be able to apply prior learning to the understanding of new skills.

One of the focal efforts in instructional placement is to establish the location of the student's acquired skill base through diagnostic testing. After this is accomplished, placement in instructional programs is established at the first unlearned skill after the base. In this placement position, the student begins instructional activities with a background of successful experiences behind him and a readiness for the skill he is about to undertake.

Several examples of students' acquired skill bases are illustrated in figure 5, which depicts a placement matrix compiled on the basis

Fig. 5
Placement Matrix Skills 1 to 32:
Each Skill Tested by Three Separate Items

Students 1 to 45

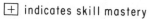

☐+ indicates skill mastery

☐− indicates skill nonmastery

☐ indicates no response

■ indicates suggested (tentative) placement position

of diagnostic test results (criterion-referenced) gathered on forty-five students. Each skill (1 to 32 along the horizontal) was represented by three test items. Students (1 to 45 along the vertical) who responded incorrectly to two or more test items for any skill received a minus (−) in the box for that skill. (Blank spaces indicate no response and are considered incorrect answers.) Two or more correct items for any skill was denoted by a plus (+). Three skills answered incorrectly in sequence (for example, − − −) indicated that the student had reached his placement position, and this was denoted by a blacked square. The blacked square was placed at the *first* of the three skills successively answered incorrectly.

An examination of the placement matrix shows that, with few exceptions, the students' placement positions were affixed just *beyond* collections of skills on which students have demonstrated a high degree of mastery. Also, with few exceptions, the instructional placement positions are at points *prior to* collections of skills on which students have demonstrated a high degree of nonmastery. In most instances, the assigned placement positions are located at points just following the students' acquired skill bases, and there is strong evidence to indicate that the students would benefit from beginning instruction at the specified placement position rather than at some more advanced position. In the case of some students, there is some evidence to indicate that the students' true placement positions may precede the suggested placement position (e.g. Students 5, 10, 16, 18, 23, 30, 33, and 40) due to erratic skill performance prior to suggested placement. Adjustments in instructional placement can be completed by the teacher after a more extensive examination of each student's test document, his item responses, and the relationship of skills, if any, which were answered incorrectly. A more detailed analysis on making decisions about placement is presented later in the chapter.

Identification of Skill Weaknesses. Accurate instructional placement assists in the identification of skill weaknesses occurring before the placement position that may require correction or supplementation if students are to make satisfactory instructional progress.

In some instances, there are groups of skills or skill strands woven throughout programs with which students have recurring problems but which are not sufficiently severe or occur so spasmodically that they do not affect placement. Consequently they are not treated. These recurring problems may never cause student failure in a program, but they can cause consistently mediocre performances that both students and teachers find inexplicable and distressing. The diagnostic and placement results of Student 33 (figure 5) provide an example of a student with several apparent skill weaknesses that exist prior to the suggested placement position. The skill weaknesses apparently were not critical enough to cause placement earlier than skill 22, but nonetheless, they may have a direct bearing on how well the student will perform in more difficult skills that will follow at this grade level or at higher grade levels.

	1	2	3	4	5	6	7	8	9	10	11	12	13	14	15	16	17	18	19	20	21	22
Student 33	+	+	+	+	−	−	+	−	+	+	+	+	+	−	+	−	+	−	−	+	−	■

Knowledge of both the student's correct placement position and skill weaknesses that exist before the suggested placement position permits the teacher to initiate instruction at a point where continuing learning gains can be made, while, at the same time, efforts can be started to reduce or eliminate nagging, lesser skill weaknesses that occurred earlier in the program foundation.

Elimination of Extraneous Variables. Locating students' correct placement positions is a critical determinant in eliminating extraneous variables from the classroom teacher's consideration when instructing students.

When correct instructional placement is not ascertained, there is an increased probability that some students' learning processes will break down with greater frequency than if they were correctly placed. Even the best developed and delivered techniques and materials often do not work, and students may fail to grasp any overall direction for or logic to programs. Instruction is reduced to a predictable sequence: skill introduction, failure, supplementation, apparent mastery, forgetting, skill introduction.... Such a sequence of events is understandable because incorrect placement generally is followed with instruction oriented toward skills about which students have no knowledge or to resolve skill weaknesses that were caused by earlier, *undetected* skill deficiencies. In these instances, instruction is focusing on extraneous skills that probably cannot be mastered because the primary skill weaknesses have still not been located.

An examination of the diagnostic and placement results of Student 12 (see figure 5) illustrates the value of accurate instructional placement in eliminating extraneous skill variables. Student 12 is about to enter a mathematics program at grade nine. The first skill to which he would normally be introduced (on the first few pages of the grade nine textbook) would be skill 16 (on this particular criterion-referenced test). According to the criterion-referenced test results below, such a placement would be inaccurate by some eleven skills. That is, the assumed (or estimated) placement position is eleven skills beyond the correct placement position. Between the two placement positions are eight skills on which the student has demonstrated nonmastery by either answering test items incorrectly or failing to answer them at all. Based on an examination of his unmastered skills, it is virtually impossible for him to succeed in the more difficult skills beginning at ninth grade. Under these conditions, instruction will be followed by failure. The failure will most likely have no correlation to teacher technique or instructional materials. It will be closely related to the fact that the skill introduced is extraneous to the student's present skill base, and no learning transfer or application can be made.

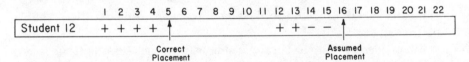

Assistance in Establishing Instructional Groups. Instructional grouping patterns can be more readily established in school systems where expert placement data have been gathered. Using individual student placement information, it is a simple matter for classroom teachers to group students for instruction according to their placement locations and skill weaknesses. The teacher receives two immediate and direct benefits from placement data that help establish instructional groups: time is conserved when all students in groups are at or near the same placements because skills delivered are appropriate for all of the students; and students can interact with and reinforce one another without the problems inherent in having very slow or very rapid students as group members.

Figure 6 suggests the placement positions of twenty-five students enrolled in a wood shop class after criterion-referenced testing. How the teacher finally groups the students for instruction will be dependent upon any number of variables including the type of program operated in the classroom, the degree to which student rates of learning will be controlled, the results of detailed test examination, and a host of other variables that the teacher may wish to consider. Nonetheless, placement information derived from diagnostic testing has provided the teacher with an assessment of the students' learning strengths, weaknesses, and placements, and he will be able to group the students on any or all of these criteria or on the basis of select learning activities. Further, the testing and placement results if expertly applied will greatly increase the effectiveness of instruction to each group and the student communication within each group. Whatever final pattern the teacher determines appropriate for his classroom, instructional placement data insure that grouping judgments can be made accurately and quickly.

Assistance in Selecting Appropriate Instructional Materials. School systems that have program foundations specified and cross-referenced to instructional materials can use placement data to assist classroom teachers in locating appropriate classroom materials. Knowledge of a student's placement position and earlier skill weaknesses—coupled with a reference for locating those skills in school system texts and materials—minimizes improper material selection and greatly increases the speed with which a learning problem can be remedied with exemplary instructional presentations and materials.

Conservation of Time. Time is a most important scarce commodity to classroom teachers. Activities that can conserve teachers' time by increasing the efficiency with which instructional processes are carried out will have a direct effect on the overall quality and quantity of services that students receive. Correct placement has a significant impact on the conservation of time. In each instance where students have been placed correctly, teacher time is saved in quickly locating appropriate instructional materials, grouping, eliminating the instruction of previously mastered skills, avoiding the instruc-

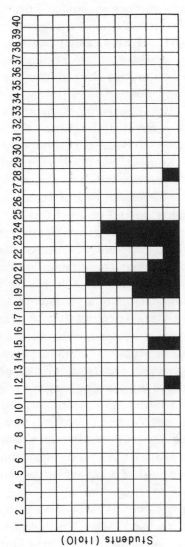

Fig. 6
Distribution of Placements: Skills 1 to 40

tion of extraneous advanced skills when earlier skills have not been acquired, determining preplacement skill weaknesses, and preparing for instructional presentation. In a similar manner student time is being saved. Correct placement insures that students will neither be overplaced (in skills far too difficult) nor underplaced (in skills already mastered). Both types of placements often result in failure, boredom, and far less skill acquisition than could be achieved if correct placement had been accomplished originally. Correct placement increases the probability that students' time will be used efficiently and effectively to enhance their learning progress.

Reduction of Student Frustration. A value of accurate placement that cannot readily be assessed is the reduction of student frustration that occurs when instruction is carried out at a point that is meaningful for the student. Nonetheless, few would question that students enjoy involvement in school programs far less when they are failing because of drastic errors in placement or they are forced to relearn content areas that are simple or blatantly obvious even before instruction. Correct placement enhances the prospects that slower students will not be overmatched in instructional programs and frustrated by the complexity of classroom content. At the same time, brighter, more insightful students will not be undermatched and bored by plodding, unimaginative programs that crush all incentive for creative initiative and advanced learning.

Specification of Need for Curricular Revision. Group diagnostic, placement, and preplacement data frequently yield valuable information about the quality of a program's skill content, sequencing, and rationale. Occasionally such data pinpoint seemingly unnecessary program skills, skills that are out of sequence, transitional skills that do not fulfill their intended function of helping the student bridge one skill to the next, unnecessary skill repetition, skill groupings that are too broad and should be subdivided for both instructional and testing purposes, poor test items, inadequate instructional materials, and, on occasion, poor instruction. Placement information collected from criterion-referenced test instruments can play a viable role in school system curricular revision and foster a more critical analysis and justification of the design and content of local programs. For example, school systems would do well to examine the content, logic, and placement of Skill 5 illustrated on the earlier placement matrix (figure 5). Considering that twenty-seven out of forty-five students responded incorrectly to this skill and only two students' placements were affected by the incorrect responses there is substantial cause to be skeptical about (1) the skill's relationship to other, immediately higher level skills, (2) the skill's location at that point in the program, (3) the redeeming value of the skill at any point in the program, (4) the materials used to teach that skill, (5) the items used to test the skill, and a number of similar concerns. Whether or not educators finally do make adjustments to their programs after examining placement data, they will be in an undeniably more secure position to justify what is or is not being done. Diagnostic and placement information provides the tools for such critical program analyses.

Projection of Need for Designing Flexible Instructional Programs. Often educators extoll the virtues of individualized instruction or continuous progress education programs without seriously attempting to establish such programs. Placement information firmly establishes the *need* for such programs beyond any questionable doubt.

Like other formal organizations, school systems change slowly and only after internal opposition. Designing flexible curricular programs ranks high as a stated "desirable" change in school systems, but in reality there is much opposition to such programs from many administrators and teachers. Too frequently educators will refuse to develop flexible, individualized instruction approaches even though many students are failing. At the same time, the opponents of flexible instructional programs may outspokenly criticize school system efforts to develop more sophisticated diagnostic, placement, and instruction tools as being unnecessary "research work" or invasions of the "academic freedom" of professional educators. Sound placement information can clearly establish that students do vary in their abilities to cope with instructional programs. Further, it can furnish the sound, factual data required to refute the notion that students will all succeed in programs that have arbitrarily fixed standard placement positions, learning rates, and instructional materials for students of varied abilities. In the face of sound student placement information, an argument in opposition to the design of flexible instructional programs is a position favoring the certain failure of substantial numbers of school system students.

Designing Effective Instructional Systems

The effectiveness of a local school system's design of an instructional placement system will be dependent upon the previous development of program foundations and criterion-referenced tests. In the absence of either or both of these tools, student placement is a difficult and, most often, a faulty process. The necessary components of an instructional placement system are standard for most school systems. Basic to each system are (1) instructional program foundations, (2) criterion-referenced tests, (3) placement parameters, (4) procedures for interpreting and using placement data, (5) grouping guidelines, (6) back-up testing systems, (7) references to program skill content, and (8) program skill cross-referencing.

Instructional Program Foundations. The primary purpose of an instructional placement system is to permit teachers to link student diagnostic test data to instructional program foundations. Obviously, instructional program foundations must be clearly specified. This insures that students' skill weaknesses can be found in the school system's texts and other materials, and instruction can be delivered that is immediately on target. Teachers should not be made to guess the identity, significance, or location of program skills that have been tested and will affect placement and instruction.

Criterion-Referenced Tests. Accurate placement requires the availability of diagnostic instruments that can assess student strengths and weaknesses and match them with the instructional program foundations unique to a given school system. The diagnostic tests will need to be criterion-referenced to yield information consistent with the school system's unique skills, skill sequence, priorities, instructional format, and program offerings.

As with the availability of previously designed instructional program foundations, criterion-referenced tests speed the placement process by eliminating teacher guesswork and search activities. They pinpoint explicit skill weaknesses by grade level, specific skill name, type, and location. These skill weaknesses are, in turn, located in the instructional program foundations. Their identification is reliable because the test's content and sequence is designed to reflect the specific content of the foundations.

Placement Parameters. Each school system that has developed instructional program foundations and criterion-referenced tests will need to establish its own parameters for placing students. Placement parameters are the operational procedures for determining the point in an instructional program foundation beyond which a student should not be placed. The purpose of setting placement parameters is to reduce the possibility of student failure through misplacement. This is accomplished by specifying the school system's or program's tolerance (parameters) for incorrect responses by students on diagnostic tests. Placement of students beyond the parameters increases the likelihood of failure. Thus, placement parameters, if finely and logically derived, should serve much the same functions as a bookmaker's odds at the race track or a life insurance company's actuarial tables in furnishing reliable estimations on the probability that a student will or will not fail if placement is beyond the recommended position. In instances where instructional placement parameters are followed, there is no guarantee that students will succeed, of course, but the probability of success is increased. On the other hand, ignoring well-designed and logically conceived parameters and placing students beyond their suggested placement positions dramatically increases the probability of instructional failure.

Placement parameters generally specify that students should be placed at a skill level prior to a point where they began demonstrating successive incorrect responses on test items. As an example, teachers and test designers may stipulate that students will be placed on the first skill of the earliest three skills that are answered incorrectly. Thus, at any point in testing where a student answers three skills incorrectly in sequence, he will be placed in instructional materials representing the first of those three skills. This represents one set of placement parameters.

```
Skills        1  2  3  4  5  6  7  8  9 10 11 12
Responses     +  +  -  +  +  -  +  -  -  -  +  -
Placement                          ↑
```

Placement parameters vary with the type of program or course in which diagnosis is undertaken and, also, with the program course skill relationships. Hierarchical and cyclical programs normally have placement based on a number of successive incorrect responses because the programs are sequenced and mastery of one skill is dependent upon prior mastery of other skills. With these types of skill relationships, placement is relatively easy to locate. The teacher need only look for the first series of incorrect test item responses that fit the established parameters and place the student at the first skill in the sequence of faulty responses.

```
Skills        1  2  3  4  5  6  7  8  9 10 11 12 13 14
Responses     +  -  +  +  +  -  +  -  -  -  +  -  -  -
Placement                          ↑
```

Placement parameters designed for unitized skill relationships will vary only slightly from those used in hierarchical or cyclical relationships. Though skills are blocked in units that may be unrelated to one another and afford little or no learning transfer from one unit to the next, an examination of successive incorrect test item responses *within a unit*—where skills are often hierarchically sequenced and closely related—will yield conclusive and usable placement information. This procedure is most satisfactory for determining placement within a unit of skills. The principles applicable to hierarchical or cyclical programs are then applied to each unit independently of previous units. By establishing the number of skills answered incorrectly in sequence or totally within a unit and comparing the results to established placement parameters, students may be placed at the first missed skill or cluster of skills within the unit. An illustration is provided where the placement parameters are: three skill errors within a unit signify that placement should begin with the first skill missed in that unit.

```
Skils        A  B  C  D  E     L  M  N  O  P  Q     F  G  H  I  J  W  X  Y  Z
Responses    +  +  -  +  -     -  -  +  +  +  +     -  +  -  -  -  +  -  +  -
Placement                                              ↑
```

In random skill relationships, a series of successive incorrect answers on skill test items has less meaning than in the three previous skill relationships. Nonetheless, test items answered incorrectly are still the primary basis for determining student placement. In these programs, placement parameters may be set to determine the number or percentage of incorrect responses to test items covering a set number of skills. For example, teachers and test designers may state that at any point in a test where the student scores 5 out of 8 items incorrectly placement will be established at the first skill (within those eight skills) where the student responded incorrectly. In this instance, placement is based on an excessively high incidence of failure on skills that have a similar level of difficulty. An illustration of the application of this placement parameter to a random skill relationship is provided.

```
Skills       1  2  3  4  5  6  7  8  9  10 11 12 13 14
Responses    +  -  +  +  -  +  -  +  -  +  -  -  +  -
Placement              ↑
```

The stringency of placement parameters is an option that is exercised by local teachers and test designers. The more restrictive are placement parameters the less chance is there that students will be overplaced. At the same time, overly stringent parameters increase the probability that larger numbers of students will be underplaced. For example, a placement parameter requiring near perfection from students being tested (90 percent accuracy or greater) may well cause students to be placed in instructional materials that have been previously mastered and are a part of the acquired skill base. Such high parameters do not allow any margin of student error or forgetting in test taking.

Some reasonable balance between permissive and stringent parameters should be sought, and setting them, like many other educational activities, will require at least some experimentation by administrators and teachers. A reasonable placement parameter in second grade reading may not be reasonable at all in tenth grade history. Nonetheless, a fairly safe beginning set of placement parameters may be between three and five skills answered incorrectly in succession, with a majority of the test items representing each skill answered incorrectly. From that point, parameters can be adjusted on the basis of observed student performances in instruction and testing after placement. If subsequent information indicates the parameters are too permissive or stringent, adjustments then can be made.

Procedures for Placement Data Interpretation and Usage. With the administration of criterion-referenced tests and the application

Fig. 7
Procedures for Interpreting and Using Diagnostic and Placement Information

Individual Diagnostic Inventory Example
Test Form MA K1–9

Washington Elementary
Class K-2
Sullivan, Monique

ARITHMETIC COMPUTATION

Q#01	Q#02	Q#03	Q#04	Q#05	Q#06	Q#07	Q#08	Q#09	Q#10	Q#11
+	+	+	+	+	+	+	+	−	+	+

Q#12	Q#13	Q#14	Q#15	Q#16	Q#17	Q#18	Q#19	Q#20	Q#21	Q#22
+	+	+		+	−	−	−	−	+	+

Q#23	Q#24	Q#25	Q#26	Q#27	Q#28	Q#29	Q#30	Q#31	Q#32
−	−	+	−	+	+	−	−	−	+

SKILL PLACEMENT MA151-060   QUESTION NUMBER 17
EQUATION, ZERO, AND VERTICAL NOTATION

GEOMETRY

Q#33	Q#34	Q#35	Q#36	Q#37
I	I	I	+	+

SKILL PLACEMENT MASTERY

MONEY

Q#38	Q#39	Q#40
+	−	

TIME

Q#41
+

RESPONSE KEY
+ = MASTERY OF SKILL
− = NONMASTERY OF SKILL
(blank) = RESPONSE OMITTED

A Guide to Classroom Teachers

1. You have before you a set of tests and results for the students in your class. The tests are criterion-referenced. That means they are constructed on our school system's skills. Therefore, they give explicit

information on how well "our" students performed on "our" skills. They provide a means of correctly diagnosing and placing students in "our" programs.

2. The administration of the criterion-referenced tests furnishes a skill assessment of each student. Skill strengths, weaknesses, and areas of questionable strength are identified.

3. The test data indicate each student's placement position and skills that may need to be reviewed.

4. Examine the "individual diagnostic inventory" (see example). This inventory depicts individual student performance on the criterion-referenced test that was administered.

5. A positive sign (+) indicates that the student has responded correctly to at least two of the three items representing that skill on the test. A positive sign means that there is a high probability that the student knows this skill.

6. A negative sign (−) indicates that the student has responded incorrectly to at least two of the three items representing that skill on the test. A negative sign means that there is a high probability that the student does not know this skill.

7. A blank space indicates that the student has not responded to any or a majority of the items representing that skill on the test. A blank space means that there is a high probability that the student does not know this skill.

8. At the middle of the individual diagnostic inventory, you will see the words SKILL PLACEMENT. This is followed by a number (for example, MA 151-060) that is a special coding depicting the skill·in which the student should be placed in the instructional program. Following the skill placement number is a reference to the test items which represented this skill on the test (for example, QUESTION NUMBER 17). Immediately below the skill placement number is the name of the skill where the student will be placed (for example, EQUATION, ZERO, AND VERTICAL NOTATION).

9. How is the student's placement position determined? It is determined on the basis of successive incorrect responses to test items. In this instance, the first three skills that are answered incorrectly *in succession* (each skill is represented by three test items) establish that the student will be placed at the *first* of the three skills successively answered incorrectly. The student will have answered a minimum of two test items incorrectly on each of those three skills or a total of six to nine items wrong out of nine items.

10. After the placement position of each student is reviewed, you may find it valuable to develop a skill placement matrix for all of the students in your class. This can be done by listing skill names (or numbers) along the top of a sheet of paper and the names of students down the left hand margin. Then, from left to right, the students' responses to each skill can be inserted.

Skill	1	2	3	4	5	6	7	8	9	10	11	12	13
Names:													
Abbott, Melissa	+	+	−	+	+	+	[−]	−	−		−	+	−
Boyle, Kim	−	+	−	+	+	+	[+	−]	−	−		−	
Cannon, Tod	−	+	−	+	+	+	+	+	−	+	[−]	−	−

The matrix will provide a visual picture of the placement of all students in the classroom. It will also illustrate each skill weakness that is common to several students (for example, Skill 3). Thus, it has value for grouping students for supplemental or reinforcement instruction.

11. After you have completed the placement matrix from information contained on all of your students' individual diagnostic inventories, you are able to group students who have skill placement positions fairly close to one another.

12. Then determine the skill placement position where all of the members of each group will begin in the instructional program foundation.

13. Select representative instructional materials to teach the skills to the students in each of the groups.

14. If possible, test the students in each group before beginning instruction to reaffirm that the data gathered from the criterion-referenced test are conclusive. A single skill test of eight to ten times for each group should be sufficient for this purpose. (The teacher will remember that only three test items represent each skill on the criterion-referenced test. Pretesting with a single-skill test of substantially greater item content is intended to reaffirm or refute the accuracy of the skill placement position prescribed by the criterion-referenced test.)

15. Presuming that students do poorly on the single-skill test, place the students (and groups) in selected instructional materials and begin instruction.

16. As time permits, you may find it beneficial to construct skill building folders for work with students who have exhibited weaknesses on skills that occurred prior to their placement positions. Because these skills had little or only a marginal effect on final placement, there is no immediate concern for early supplementation or reinforcement. Nonetheless, reinforcement should take place at some future time, and prepared folders containing representative instructional materials can be valuable for casual introduction of troublesome skills. This skill supplementation may prevent future instructional failure and most likely will improve students' general preparedness for subsequent learning.

of placement parameters, teachers will receive information for placing students in instructional programs. From this information, they must initiate final placement activities in preparation for instruction. Written procedures for interpreting and using placement data serve as a necessary aid to guide teachers in these activities. They explain the type of information the teacher will receive, the purpose of the information, application of it, and general suggestions. The procedures should be clear, uncluttered, and put the teacher at ease in reviewing criterion-referenced test documents and placement data, establishing instructional groups, locating individual or group placement on the instructional program foundation, selecting materials, and initiating instruction. In figure 7 a diagnostic document titled "individual diagnostic inventory" is detailed to illustrate the performance of one student on a criterion-referenced test. This is followed by a sample set of procedures for interpreting and using the diagnostic and placement information contained on the individual diagnostic inventory.

Grouping Guidelines. Sophisticated and sensitive criterion-referenced test instruments increase the accuracy of instructional placement to a point almost unimaginable in most school systems. Such accuracy increases the probability that most students will succeed if sound instruction is provided at designated placement positions. This placement accuracy, however, introduces a serious problem for classroom teachers: instructional management becomes an increasingly more complex problem with which to cope. Classroom teachers who normally conduct instruction within the framework of one to three groups may quickly find that test data specify the need for three, four, or more groups within the classroom. The teacher may be willing to concede the necessity of more instructional groups and may even agree to a modest increase in the number of groups, but some guidance must be available for helping to set the number of groups at a manageable number while insuring that no student will fail because of overplacement. If this is not done, the teacher may become frustrated, disgruntled, and fail or students may receive poor instruction. In this instance, grouping guidelines are necessary to help the teacher arrive at a best grouping arrangement that will prevent student failure and insure good, though not maximal, student achievement gains. Figure 8 illustrates the placement positions of thirty-eight students tested with a criterion-referenced test. It is followed by a set of procedures that details how the teacher may organize these students in groups to undertake instruction.

Educators will recognize that the implementation of grouping

Fig. 8
Procedures for Student Grouping

A Guide to Classroom Teachers

1. Examine criterion-referenced test documents and individual diagnostic inventories for each student in the class.
2. Examine suggested instructional placement positions of each student in the class on the class grouping report or, if such a report is not available, list in sequence the instructional placement positions of each student in the class.

Wanda Anderson	MA 101-005
Cecil Darby	MA 101-045
Cindi Michaels	MA 101-055
Calvin Dawkins	MA 101-055

3. Determine those students who are to be placed in instructional skills *below* grade level. Meet with other teachers who instruct the same or lower grade levels and initiate procedures for cross-grade level or cross-unit grouping, involving the exchange of students from one grade level or instructional group to another.
4. Determine those students who are to be placed in instructional skills *above* grade level. Meet with other teachers who instruct the same or higher grade levels and initiate procedures for cross-grade level or cross-unit grouping, involving the exchange of students from one grade level or instructional group to another.
5. Determine the number of different placement positions or potential groupings that are located *on* your grade level.
6. Meet with grade level colleagues and ascertain the number and type of different instructional placement positions or potential groupings that are located on your grade level. Initiate procedures for intragrade level exchange of students from one classroom or instructional group to another.
7. Redetermine the numbers of different placement positions or potential groupings that will be located in your classroom.
8. Determine the number of different placement positions or potential groupings that you can or will manage.
9. Select strategic skill placement positions at or near ranges of skills in which substantial numbers of students have been designated for placement. Group the students at the lowest unmastered skill exhibited by the most deficient student. Repeat this process until the number of groupings exist that the classroom teacher specified was manageable.

Individual Placement Position	Frequency	Group Placement Position
MA 151-045	3	MA 151-045
MA 151-050	6	MA 151-045
MA 151-055	1	MA 151-045

10. Begin instruction.
11. Maintain controlled learning rate.

Class Grouping Report: Test Form MA K1-9

My class √ (originally)
To Miss Anderson's class   = 1
To Mr. Robert's class   = 2
From Miss Anderson's class = 3
From Mr. Robert's class   = 4

Washington Elementary
Class K-2

	Student Name	Skill Placement	Skill Name
1	W.A.√	MA-101-005	PRE-READINESS—SET RECOGNITION
1	C.D.√	MA-101-045	PRE-READINESS—ORDERING, CLASSIFYING, AND COMPARING SETS
1	C.M.√	MA-101-055	SPATIAL RELATIONSHIPS
1	C.D.√	MA-101-055	SPATIAL RELATIONSHIPS
1	I.L.√	MA-101-055	SPATIAL RELATIONSHIPS
1	I.C.√	MA-101-060	THINKING ANALYTICALLY AND CREATIVELY ABOUT PATTERNS
2	K.S.√	MA-101-065	COMPARISON OF SETS BY VISUAL INSPECTION
2	T.E.√	MA-101-065	COMPARISON OF SETS BY VISUAL INSPECTION
2	V.J.√	MA-101-065	COMPARISON OF SETS BY VISUAL INSPECTION
2	C.S.√	MA-101-070	ONE TO ONE MATCHING AND EQUIVALENT SETS
2	D.M.√	MA-101-070	ONE TO ONE MATCHING AND EQUIVALENT SETS
2	M.T.√	MA-101-075	COMPARISON OF NON-EQUIVALENT SETS AND THE CONCEPT OF ONE MORE
2	K.G.√	MA-101-140	ORDINALS

Below
Grade
Level

Grade Level		Code	Objective	
3	C.J.	MA-151-045	ORDERING THE NUMERALS ON THE NUMBER LINE	
3	D.L.	MA-151-045	ORDERING THE NUMERALS ON THE NUMBER LINE	
4	D.V.	MA-151-045	ORDERING THE NUMERALS ON THE NUMBER LINE	
	D.D.✓	MA-151-050	"GREATER THAN"—"LESS THAN" AND THE RELATED INEQUALITY SYMB	
	I.D.✓	MA-151-050	"GREATER THAN"—"LESS THAN" AND THE RELATED INEQUALITY SYMB	
3	I.T.	MA-151-050	"GREATER THAN"—"LESS THAN" AND THE RELATED INEQUALITY SYMB	Group #1
	M.D.✓	MA-151-050	"GREATER THAN"—"LESS THAN" AND THE RELATED INEQUALITY SYMB	
	Q.T.✓	MA-151-050	"GREATER THAN"—"LESS THAN" AND THE RELATED INEQUALITY SYMB	
	S.D.✓	MA-151-050	"GREATER THAN"—"LESS THAN" AND THE RELATED INEQUALITY SYMB	
3	X.T.	MA-151-055	UNION OF SETS, ADDITION AND THE PLUS SIGN	
	C.D.✓	MA-151-060	EQUATION, ZERO, AND VERTICAL NOTATION	
	G.D.✓	MA-151-060	EQUATION, ZERO, AND VERTICAL NOTATION	
4	M.S.	MA-151-060	EQUATION, ZERO, AND VERTICAL NOTATION	
4	L.T.	MA-151-060	EQUATION, ZERO, AND VERTICAL NOTATION	Group #2
	Z.B.✓	MA-151-060	EQUATION, ZERO, AND VERTICAL NOTATION	
4	H.M.	MA-151-062	SYMBOL FOR EQUALITY, EQUATION, AND ZERO	
	I.M.✓	MA-151-062	SYMBOL FOR EQUALITY, EQUATION, AND ZERO	
	M.S.✓	MA-151-062	SYMBOL FOR EQUALITY, EQUATION, AND ZERO	
4	D.T.	MA-151-065	MISSING ADDENDS IN ADDITION	
	T.C.✓	MA-151-065	MISSING ADDENDS IN ADDITION	Group #3
3	I.S.	MA-151-075	SUBTRACTIVE PROPERTY OF ZERO IN SUMS OF FIVE OR LESS	
	B.Y.✓	MA-151-080	MISSING ADDENDS AND SUMS IN SUBTRACTION	
4	E.W.	MA-151-080	MISSING ADDENDS AND SUMS IN SUBTRACTION	
3	H.S.	MA-151-080	MISSING ADDENDS AND SUMS IN SUBTRACTION	
4	S.S.	MA-151-085	INVERSE RELATIONS—WITH SUMS AND DIFFERENCES OF FIVE OR LESS	Group #4

On Grade Level

guidelines such as those suggested above will curb achievement gains for some students. This is a temporary intended restriction because unbridled progress by students in open-ended individualized instruction programs can quickly destroy original instructional groupings established by classroom teachers. If some semblance of control is not temporarily maintained on the progress of individuals within the instructional groupings, teachers will be frustrated with the massive management problems that evolve in the classroom. This frustration, if permitted to build, will cause disenchantment with the criterion-referenced diagnosis, placement, and instruction process. Eventually, sound diagnostic and placement activities will be stopped, or the results of such activities will be ignored or rationalized to conform to pre-established placement patterns that are workable but not necessarily in keeping with collected diagnostic findings. Such an occurrence is defeating for teachers, students, and the school system. This is intentionally prevented by the use of grouping guidelines until teachers feel comfortable with managing larger numbers of groups. Grouping guidelines can be slowly altered as teacher confidence builds and the number of groups increased until most students will be learning in smaller groups or individual settings at rates of learning, levels of abstraction, and placement positions commensurate with their individual abilities. Hypothetically, all students will then be given the encouragement and latitude to learn to their maximal potential. The conditions will be conducive to this form of instruction, and teachers will support and promote them. This last point—teacher support—is critical. The success of sound instructional procedures and processes is largely dependent upon classroom teachers, their acceptance, and their ability to manage instruction in the classroom. The grouping guidelines help teachers experience success in the diagnostic and placement process and arrive at the point where they have confidence that this process can facilitate exceptional learning opportunities for students and, yet, be managed.

Back-Up Testing Systems. A necessary component is designing effective instructional placement systems in a series of single-skill back-up tests. Occasionally called pretests, a back-up test system is a tool for teachers to use in reaffirming student skill strengths and weaknesses and placement positions identified in criterion-referenced testing.

Though there is little cause for questioning the diagnostic and placement effectiveness of well-designed criterion-referenced tests, classroom teachers may be concerned about the limited number of items that represent each skill on these tests. Even very detailed forms of criterion-referenced tests rarely contain more than three to five items for each skill, and some teachers may feel uncomfortable making final diagnostic and placement decisions on that small skill representation. Because developing criterion-referenced tests with broader item representation for each skill would increase test administration time, teachers may want to pretest their students with single skill tests of 8 to 20 items to reaffirm the accuracy of the suggested placement position prior to initiating instruction. Such a practice is instructionally sound and should be encouraged. The availability of a series of single-skill back-up tests will serve as an additional inducement for teachers to be vigilant about correct student diagnosis and placement and mindful of the human deficiencies that can cause criterion-referenced test data occasionally to be inaccurate.

References to Program Skill Content. As in the development of criterion-referenced tests, placement systems require that skills and test items are referenced to program content. The purpose of such referencing is to reduce the time required by teachers using information from placement documents to locate the instructional content where skill weaknesses are treated. Thus, the reference is intended to eliminate guessing about each student's placement position, the skill on which instruction is to be initiated, and the contextual location of the skill.

References to program skill content may be made directly to textbooks used by the school system; curriculum guides; or a system of learning modules, packages, or units that encompass all learning resources available to teachers. All three procedures are satisfactory; however, the latter is certainly the most encompassing. (Learning unit, module, or package development is treated in the following chapter.)

References to Program Skill Content

	Item #	Skill Name	Reference to Skill Content
Skills to Textbooks	17	Numerals 1–4	A. W., pp. 123-125
Skills to Curriculum Guide	17	Numerals 1–4	Math Guide, pp. 116-120
Skills to Learning Unit	17	Numerals 1–4	MA 151-060.00

Program Skill Cross-References. After students are successfully placed in an instructional program, there are many occasions when a teacher may want to trace a skill weakness to its origin and gather basic materials on all related skills that must be learned prior to the mastery of the skill in question. Such material location and gathering necessitate a detailed program skill cross-reference and the referencing of skills to program content. This activity is suggested for both the design of an effective instructional placement system and for constructing criterion-referenced tests.

Program skill cross-references are developed by attaching subordinate skill names or, more conveniently, skill numbers to each skill contained in the instructional program foundation, to each test item on a criterion-referenced test, or each skill module, unit, or package designed in the school system. Then, as a student is placed for instruction, the classroom teacher need only examine the instructional program foundation, test document, or curriculum system to locate (1) all subordinate, related skills and (2) the program content location of those skills.

A sample of program skill cross-reference is illustrated below.

Item #	Skill Name	Program Reference	Skill Cross-Reference
17	Numerals 1–4	MA 151-060.00	MA 151-055.00
		or	MA 151-010.00
		A.W. pp.123–125	MA 151-005.00
			MA 101-095.00
			MA 101-090.00
			MA 101-085.00

Design Work for the Teacher

Having previously completed the development of an instructional program foundation and one or more criterion-referenced tests, the design work required to determine student placement is relatively easy by comparison. Suppose that for the purposes of illustration, you have completely specified a program foundation for grades 10 and 11 English literature and constructed and administered a grade 10½ and 11½ criterion-referenced test to your eleventh grade literature class. With the corrected test results in hand, you will want to develop a placement matrix form similar to the completed one presented earlier in the chapter or like the one in the document section of this chapter. After listing student names on the placement matrix, insert the test results for each student on a skill by skill basis. Pluses, minuses, and blank spaces can be used to denote skills on which students have demonstrated mastery, nonmastery, or no responses.

Now, you will need to establish parameters for determining where students' placement positions should be located. The placement parameters will be affixed according to (1) the type of skill relationship (hierarchical, cyclical, unitized, random) around which your course is developed and (2) the permissiveness or stringency of your criteria for placing students.

Suppose that you determine that your English literature course is structured in a unitized fashion, including such units of study as the short story, poetry, biography, adventure novels, mystery novels, travel, and so forth. Each unit has several skills, concepts, and processes to be conveyed, like the author's purpose, author style, story purpose, character significance, and others. With this information, you may determine that your parameters will be established to place students on the basis of either a series of skill errors in sequence within a unit or a set percentage of skill errors in the unit. These are options that are totally open to you.

Assuming you have determined that the placement parameters will be based on a set percentage of skill errors in a unit and the percentage of error you believe to be unacceptable is 15 percent or more, each student's test responses will be examined, unit by unit, on the placement matrix. In the first unit that meets your placement cut off (15 percent or more skills are answered incorrectly), you will circle or blacken the first skill answered incorrectly in that unit. That is where the student will be tentatively placed. The identical process will then be repeated on the test item responses of the remaining students in the class. You will want to remember that placement parameters can be altered if they appear to be too permissive or stringent, but it is best to employ fairly lofty standards in their initial development. It is far better, initially, to underplace students than to overplace them. The first error may cause temporary boredom that can be eliminated later. Overplacement, on the other hand, can cause immediate student failure.

With each student's tentative placement ascertained, review (1) the procedures for interpreting and using placement data and (2) grouping guidelines presented earlier in the chapter. You may want to modify these procedures and guidelines to fit your pattern of operation, but make certain the issues discussed in them are addressed in your revised procedures and guidelines.

List each of your students' names in the sequence in which they are tentatively placed. Begin by listing the student who is placed earliest in the course and proceed to the name of the one who will be placed at the most advanced position in the course. Then, using the references (test items referenced to skills) developed in chapter 3, cite the name of the skill in which each student will be placed.

You are now prepared to group your students for instruction. Here you will want to meet with other teachers undertaking developmental activities similar to yours and discuss the possibility of cross-grade or cross-section grouping. If it is possible to implement such student exchanges for grouping purposes, management of instruction and the delivery of greater service to students is vastly enhanced.

With or without consideration being given to cross-grade or cross-section grouping, you will want to examine the grouping guidelines to help in reorganizing your class into a small number of manageable instructional groups. This may be as few as two or as many as five groups at the beginning. The members of each group will be selected on the basis of identical or fairly close placement positions. Determinations on which group a student on the borderline between two groups should be placed will be dependent upon (1) the closeness or similarity of his placement skill to the types of skills being taught to members of each of the groups, (2) his skill weaknesses prior to the placement skill, and (3) finally, the sizes of the two groups.

After each student has been placed in a group, each of the groups will begin instruction on the skill that its least advanced student has not mastered. This will insure you that you are working with only the original established two to five groups and not trying to control other groups or individuals *within* established groups. Later, if you feel comfortable and effective in teaching larger numbers of groups, you can redivide the original groups again. That should not be done, however, until you are confident that an additional number of groups will not be unmanageable.

With each of the groups now prepared to begin instruction on a particular skill, you may want to reaffirm, indeed, that all students are placed correctly. That is, you may want to check the accuracy of the criterion-referenced test. This can be accomplished by administering a back-up test constructed solely around the placement skill of *each* group because all of the members of a group will be started in the same skill instruction. In this instance, if you have three groups, you will need three back-up tests or one for each group. The tests should include a larger number of items for the skill being assessed than the criterion-referenced test does. If the criterion-referenced test contains three items for the placement skill, you may want to use five to ten items in the back-up test.

An alternative way to check earlier criterion-referenced test results is merely to assign students a series of activities from textbooks or workbooks and have the results of these activities serve to affirm or refute the accuracy of placement. In either case, if all students accurately respond to the back-up test or assigned activities with a high degree of proficiency, the students are placed at too low a skill level. They will then need to be tested at higher skill levels until some of them cannot successfully complete the activities. Placement for the group will then be located.

Obviously if back-up testing or the completion of select activities immediately confirms that some students cannot perform the placement skill originally reported in the criterion-referenced test, you have confirmed the accuracy of the original placement position, and instruction can be started at once. (You will want to recall that some students will likely be able to demonstrate mastery on the back-up test administered to the group. This is because groups are formed from students whose suggested placement positions for skill instruction are within close proximity to one another but not identical to one another. Even so, the entire group will begin instruction on the identical placement skill as the least advanced student in the group. Thus, some students will demonstrate mastery of the skill on the back-up test, just as they previously demonstrated mastery on the criterion-referenced test administered earlier. These students will be reexposed to only a few skills that were previously mastered before they reach skill areas in which, they too, are weak.)

Having completed back-up testing and reaffirmed student placement positions and groups, you can now use the references to program skill content to select and assign learning activities to the group and begin formal instruction. This topic is detailed in the following chapter.

You will want to use criterion-referenced test results and program skill cross-references to begin building individual student folders for reinforcing skill weaknesses identified prior to the student's placement position. This may be done by checking the names and locations of skill weaknesses and pulling skill materials or citing page numbers where skill materials can be found. Then, on those occasions when students with identical preplacement skill weaknesses are free for supplemental instruction, they can be gathered into a temporary skill building group, provided select instruction, and assigned materials that will strengthen identified weaknesses. This type of reinforcement can be done very effectively on an ad hoc basis. However, the availability of skill folders, information on preplacement skills, and suggested skill building groups should be planned in advance. Otherwise, it is doubtful that these activities will ever take place or that they will be so ill-organized that they become less than totally effective.

As time is available over the ensuing months, you will want to examine the original criterion-referenced test document and testing and placements results in light of the performances of your students. Review your diagnostic grid and placement matrix to begin locating skill and sequence aberrations. Look for program gaps and articulation flaws. Examine frequently missed test items to determine how many are poorly constructed. Review your placement parameters, procedures for interpreting placement data, and grouping guidelines in light of how effectively you feel students progressed after being placed. The listing of items and documents to check, review, revise, and reaffirm is lengthy. But such activities can be done in a one year period of time and they will pay substantial dividends in improving the quality of instruction.

Documents

Two placement documents are used to illustrate forms for gathering information that may be used by school systems in placing students for instruction. These augment those documents presented earlier that may be created in school systems that have developed and are relying upon instructional program foundations and criterion-referenced tests in diagnosing and placing students.

Document 7 is a placement matrix. It can be used by teachers to enter student data from the individual diagnostic inventory or criterion-referenced test. Entering each class member's data on this document, the classroom teacher can identify common student placement positions; common preplacement deficiencies; program gaps; program articulation flaws; and potential instructional program foundation weaknesses.

Document 8 is a placement frequency distribution. It displays the number of students who have a common suggested placement position; the name and number of the skill where placement is suggested for that group of students; and the location of the test items on the criterion-referenced test where the skill was tested. The placement frequency distribution is designed to assist the teacher in locating and examining test item responses that affect student placement and in establishing instructional grouping patterns (this latter activity is accomplished through the joint usage of the class grouping report illustrated earlier in the chapter and the placement frequency distribution).

Document 7
Placement Matrix

Test Form _____
Class _____
School _____

SKILL NAME/NUMBER

STUDENT NAME

	1																																				
	2																																				
	3																																				
	4																																				
	5																																				
	6																																				
	7																																				
	8																																				
	9																																				
	10																																				
	11																																				
	12																																				
	13																																				
	14																																				
	15																																				
	16																																				
	17																																				
	18																																				
	19																																				
	20																																				
	21																																				
	22																																				
	23																																				
	24																																				
	25																																				

+ indicates skill mastery
− indicates skill nonmastery
   indicates no response
■ indicates suggested (tentative) placement position

Document 8
Placement Frequency Distribution:

Test Form MA K1-9

Washington Elementary
Class K-2

ITEM CLUSTER	SKILL PLACEMENT	FREQ	SKILL NAME
1	MA-101-005	1	PRE-READINESS—SET RECOGNITION
4	MA-101-045	1	PRE-READINESS—ORDERING, CLASSIFYING, AND COMPARING SETS
5	MA-101-055	3	SPATIAL RELATIONSHIPS
6	MA-101-060	1	THINKING ANALYTICALLY AND CREATIVELY ABOUT PATTERNS
7	MA-101-065	3	COMPARISON OF SETS BY VISUAL INSPECTION
8	MA-101-070	2	ONE TO ONE MATCHING AND EQUIVALENT SETS
9	MA-101-075	1	COMPARISON OF NON-EQUIVALENT SETS AND THE CONCEPT OF ONE MORE
10	MA-101-140	1	ORDINALS
14	MA-151-045	3	ORDERING THE NUMERALS ON THE NUMBER LINE
15	MA-151-050	6	"GREATER THAN"—"LESS THAN" AND THE RELATED INEQUALITY SYMB
16	MA-151-055	1	UNION OF SETS, ADDITION AND THE PLUS SIGN
17	MA-151-060	5	EQUATION, ZERO, AND VERTICAL NOTATION
18	MA-151-062	3	SYMBOL FOR EQUALITY, EQUATION, AND ZERO
19	MA-151-065	2	MISSING ADDENDS IN ADDITION
21	MA-151-075	1	SUBTRACTIVE PROPERTY OF ZERO IN SUMS OF FIVE OR LESS
22	MA-151-080	3	MISSING ADDENDS AND SUMS IN SUBTRACTION
23	MA-151-085	1	INVERSE RELATIONS—WITH SUMS AND DIFFERENCES OF FIVE OR LESS

5.   Prescription

Prescription is the process of providing select learning activities to students at appropriate placement positions to insure the greatest probability of skill acquisition. Implicit in prescription is the diagnosis of students with criterion-referenced test instruments based upon school system program foundations and the placement and teaching of those students in a manner that is consistent with gathered diagnostic data.

The unwary may fail in differentiating between prescription and instruction. Yet, the distinction is most important in its impact upon the conduct of school system programs and the level of student learning. Instruction merely suggests the delivery of learning activities to students. Prescription connotes the presence and application of student diagnostic and placement information prior to the delivery of learning activities. It further implies that the diagnostic and placement information has played a significant role in formulating teachers' instructional plans of action and that students will be the recipients of more accurate instruction as a result. Casual observation in most school systems affirms that programs are most often instructional in nature and not prescriptive. The absence of program foundations, criterion-referenced tests, placement documents, and correlated learning activities are four reasons of considerable magnitude that explain the dearth of prescriptive programs in the United States.

Prescription Systems Defined

Prescription systems are a series of concisely designed and stated, self-contained skill units, each aimed at teaching one or more basic skills, concepts, or processes in a program foundation. A series of self-contained skill units for an entire program (for example, K-12 mathematics, K-12 science, K-12 social studies, K-12 physical education, 7-12 industrial arts, and so forth) comprises a program's prescriptive system.

In general, the contents of a skill unit are (1) a reference number that ties the skill in the instructional program foundation to criterion-referenced test items, skill sequences, placement document data, and the skill unit itself; (2) the identity of the skill treated in the unit; (3) one or more instructional objectives; (4) one or more suggested performance indicators for determining skill mastery; (5) cross-referenced and prerequisite skills; (6) sample test items; (7) a range of learning activity references for locating the skill in school system textbooks, workbooks, materials, and media; (8) a range of worksheets for supplementing or reinforcing the skill; and (9) two or more single-skill criterion-referenced tests for assessing knowledge of a skill both before and after delivery of prescription.

The Need for Prescription Systems

If anything is clearly illustrated by a criterion-referenced diagnosis, placement, and prescriptive approach, it is that students vary in intelligence, learning rate, ability to conceptualize or deal with abstract learning activities, style of learning, and instructional placement. This variance can be affirmed time and again through the administration of nationally normed standardized achievement tests, intelligence tests, and criterion-referenced tests or through teacher observation of classroom performance.

School systems using a criterion-referenced diagnostic, placement, and prescriptive approach will need prescription systems to manage classroom activities and attend to student variances that exist.

As school systems attempt to deal with the range of student ability, teachers will need access to textbooks, workbooks, materials, and audio-visuals from which students can receive prescriptions after the completion of diagnosis and placement. Further, back-up tests, supplemental learning activities, and answer keys need to be available for follow-up. The search time for locating references or materials must be short, learning activities predesigned and pretested, a multitude of alternative learning activities available, and the skill units sequenced to match the entire span of the program foundation.

Prescription systems require painstaking design, but they are imperatives if classroom teachers are to establish and manage multiple groupings of students and deliver an array of learning activities that will help them progress satisfactorily in school programs. Obviously, the development of prescriptive systems is far more time consuming and costly than the mere delivery of programs that arbitrarily assign students for instruction without regard to learning differences. Nonetheless, if success for students is a primary goal for school systems, it is requisite that programs be prescriptively designed—sensitive to the normal distribution of students' abilities to learn and able to be adjusted to all forms of learner variability.

The Values of Prescription Systems

Prescription systems have numerous values for classroom teachers in delivering learning activities to students. The primary values of prescription systems are the effect they have on (1) classroom planning and management, (2) student achievement, and (3) the humanization of instruction.

Classroom Planning and Management. When coupled with the prior design of program foundations, criterion-referenced tests, and student placement documents, prescription systems are an immensely valuable tool for planning and managing classroom activities. Among advantages that accrue to the teacher having access to sequenced, skill-based prescriptive systems are (1) increased short- and long-range direction for the program; (2) reduced time spent in student placement and grouping; (3) access to prepared materials to carry out individualized instruction; (4) reduced time spent in determining student prescription; (5) increased flexibility in allocating planning time; and (6) increased direction for classroom assistants.

(1) Because a prescription system encompasses the entire span of a school system's program foundation, teachers are in advantaged positions to view skills and learning activities, which students previously experienced or which they will experience after they progress to a higher grade level or more advanced course. From this perspective, short- and long-range directions for the program can be used in preparing learning experiences that will assist students in skill acquisition. In other instances, some students' placement positions will fall below or above the grade level in which they are enrolled. The teacher will need information about the skills taught at the lower (or higher) grade level, names of textbooks and workbooks available for prescription, book and page number references where activities may be found, and test inventories for assessing skill mastery. These will all be readily available for planning purposes if the school system has predesigned a prescription system.

(2) Teachers expend less time placing and grouping students when prescription systems are available to them. Normally, teachers do not have criterion-referenced test data, placement documents, or prescription systems for placing and grouping students. As such, trial and error judgments must be made to determine students' skill strengths and weaknesses, and groupings are established on the basis of commonly perceived skill weaknesses. Unfortunately, students may exhibit common skill deficiencies but have very uncommon placement positions in a program, and teachers have to find this out by trial prescription. This requires the design of sets of learning activities that are specially tailored to individuals or small groups. Often as not, trial prescriptions are inaccurate, and teachers find it necessary to replace and regroup some students again and again. Each replacement, regrouping, and trial prescription development consumes valuable time that could be spent in more constructive activity. The drain that faulty placement, grouping, and prescription writing puts on teachers' time is often sufficient enough to reduce the effectiveness of classroom planning and management or cause even the most conscientious teachers to give up attempts at individualizing instruction.

(3) The availability of prescription systems increases the probability that teachers will carry out individualized instruction or con-

tinuous progress education programs. In view of the previous design of accurate diagnostic and placement instruments, the lack of a prescriptive system to initiate and to sustain an individualized instruction program prevents many teachers from delivering such programs to students. That is understandable. For example, imagine the conduct of a course or class offering in which four distinct groups of students were identified. The probable number of prescriptions, references, and tests the teacher would need to create or to locate in order to carry out an individualized instruction program—a necessity to insure the appropriate delivery of services to students—could be staggering. Worse, this developmental task would have to be maintained throughout the 180 day school year if students were to benefit from the program and progress. Then, too, the teacher may face students whose placement positions are either below or above the hypothetical skill "bounds" of the course or class being taught. In this instance, the teacher would need to design materials from textual and workbook materials used in other courses or grade levels (with which he or she may not be entirely familiar). Finally, the teacher would have to apply this effort to other classes he or she may teach. The prospect of individualized instruction occurring under those conditions is not good.

The probability of individualized instruction occurring is greatly enhanced in school systems where prescription systems are available. In these school systems, teachers need merely select textual or workbook references and ready-made prescriptive worksheets, materials, or tests and introduce them to students. Naturally, the teacher may yet design an unlimited number of prescriptions to suit his or her particular desire; but this becomes a matter of choice, not one of necessity.

(4) Prescription systems contain a multitude of varied learning activities that can be assigned to students. Thus, if some prescriptions are obviously unsatisfactory for use with some students, alternative ones are available. As one might suspect, finding the most desirable prescription requires at least some experimentation with the available alternatives. Some students function well in visual materials, some only with ones of an auditory or tactal kinesthetic orientation, some with any type of material as long as vocabulary level is controlled, and some with all types of material. Accessibility to prescription systems permits teachers to project the type of pre-

scriptions with which students will be successful, quickly test out their projections, and, then, deliver programs using materials of a design with which students have demonstrated an ability to perform successfully.

(5) Any time classroom teachers can accomplish critical diagnosis, placement, grouping, and prescription tasks with greater rapidity than previously, they are in a better position to reallocate their time to sophisticated classroom planning and management activities. Prescription systems are time savers. They reduce guesswork, error, basic design work, material organization, prescription location, and a number of other time-consuming activities. The time teachers conserve in using prescription systems can be redirected to the elimination of preplacement deficiencies, increasing the effectiveness of grouping procedures, expanding the quality or content of prescriptions, increasing one-to-one interaction with students, improving student assessment practices, and a number of other activities that will increase both teacher and student performance. The level of sophistication of classroom operation brought about by the reallocation of teacher planning time will, in turn, free even greater amounts of time for planning and organization of prescriptive activities.

(6) Prescription systems can be used by the teacher as a training or guidance device with assistants who function in the classroom. Many teachers have practice or student teachers, volunteer parents, aides, paraprofessionals, intern teachers, upper grade level students, or student helpers who work with small groups or individuals in remedial or supplemental activities. Such help is valued by the teacher, but preparing and guiding inexperienced classroom assistants is often time-consuming and reduces the time that the teacher can spend with students who need assistance. Prescription systems can be used by teachers in preparing and guiding classroom assistants. They can furnish specific directions on the presentation and assessment of program skills, and they are generally sufficiently explicit and uncomplicated to be understood by nearly any assistant the teacher may have working with students. With detailed review of the contents of a prescription system and direction from the classroom teacher, classroom assistants can function successfully with small groups of students and measurably improve the quality and quantity of skill acquisition that takes place in the classroom.

Student Achievement. The primary goal of school systems is to maximize achievement gains for students. Among the values of a prescription system is the potential it holds for increasing such gains for students. Prescription systems aid school systems in achieving this goal through (1) proper placement; (2) program articulation; (3) instructional independence; (4) advanced placement; and (5) early program completion.

(1) Perhaps the one point where school systems experience their greatest achievement losses is in misplacing students. Every student who is overplaced for instruction (placed in a program at some point beyond his acquired skill base) is an achievement risk, and most probably he will achieve somewhat or substantially less than he could if he were correctly placed. At the same time, every student who is underplaced for instruction (placed in a program at some point within his acquired skill base) is at least a temporary achievement risk, and he will relearn skills that he has previously acquired. In both instances, students and the school system are realizing moderate or substantial achievement losses that could be eliminated through correct diagnosis, placement, and prescription. Program foundations, criterion-referenced tests, and diagnostic and placement documents are not sufficient in themselves to eliminate achievement losses due to improper placement. The teacher must also be able to prescribe appropriate learning activities to the student and manage the learning process. Otherwise, early diagnostic and placement efforts may be undone through improper material selection and presentation; insufficient monitoring; misgrouping; or a failure to recognize the need for individualized instruction. Prescription systems insure that proper diagnosis and placement are followed by appropriate delivery of learning activities. They certify that students will be placed just beyond their acquired skill bases and learning activities will be correlated to the school system's program foundations. In this environment, the probability of increased student achievement is dramatically enhanced.

(2) Prescription systems assist in maximizing school system and student achievement by eliminating program, grade level, and school level articulation problems. Once students are properly placed, prescription systems affirm the continuity of learning as they progress within a program, across groups, from grade level to grade level, and from school level to school level. Prescription

systems—developed around program foundations—are devoid of unintended skill repetitions, program gaps, and foundation deficiencies. Their multigrade level design and the specificity of their written content insure that each student's placement in the system is maintained on the basis of individual progress rather than on an artificial, pre-established progress quota for a class. Presuming that there is no intentional misplacement of students and there is a total school system commitment to the diagnostic, placement, and prescriptive process, few problems should be encountered in student transition from one group, grade level, or school level to the next. In a similar manner, prescription systems provide flexibility to overcome articulation problems previously encountered when students were absent from school because of illness, work, or extended vacations. Smoothing out troublesome articulation problems in programs reduces the incidence of student misplacement and faulty prescription and increases the potential for greater student achievement gains.

(3) The content specificity and multigrade level design of prescription systems pose distinct possibilities that capable students can be given greater latitude to pursue entire programs with substantial independence of the formalized teaching-learning process. Prescription systems are sufficiently thorough for self-directed students to use them as independent study programs. After correctly placing students, teachers can provide all of the necessary prescriptive tools at hand to permit students' open-ended access to the full breadth of programs. Program skills, sequence, materials, textual references and page locations, and performance expectations are available to the student. The same materials and assessment documents are available for the teacher to use in counseling, monitoring, and assessing student progress.

Bright students who are not permitted to pursue skill acquisition vigorously or whose rates of learning are arbitrarily fixed by some class standard of progress cannot maximize their achievement. But if allowed this option, many talented students would increase their rates of learning, shorten the time spans of program completion, and experience "extra" learning activities beyond those they normally would have experienced in a structured program that did not offer independent access to program content. In these instances, both student and school system achievement are positively affected.

(4) Prescription systems provide the possibility of advanced placement for students in programs. Advanced placement recognizes that some students can demonstrate they have previously acquired skills or have the intuitive or intellectual capacity to skip over large blocks of learning activities. In this instance, prescription can begin at some point beyond where it would normally occur.

The content of prescription systems enhance the concept of advanced placement and increase the probability of greater school system and student achievement gains. With prescriptive materials previously constructed and readily accessible to teachers, students can be permitted placement at any point along a program foundation from the beginning to the end of a course, sequence of courses, or program. Because prescription systems also include back-up test instruments, students can be pretested out of previously mastered skills in program foundations and permitted to move on to skills that have not been acquired. The features of prescription systems enhance the time economy of students through advanced placement. Such economies afford students greater opportunities for increased achievement by eliminating unnecessary, repetitive prescription. Thus, the instructional independence and advanced placement capabilities of prescription systems enhance the possibility that students will complete programs earlier than would otherwise be expected. The early completion of programs affords students the opportunity to participate in and complete more courses and programs. Such options have obvious implications for maximizing student and school system achievement.

The Humanization of Instruction. Prescription systems, offering a vastly heightened probability of success for all students, are humanized in that they recognize and provide for (1) individual variances, (2) individual styles, (3) group participation, and (4) the integration of all skill classes.

(1) Program foundations, criterion-referenced tests, and diagnostic and placement documents are designed to capture information about a student's readiness for and placement in program materials. Prescription systems are designed to insure that the school system and its teachers are prepared to begin teaching students at any point along a program foundation. All four systems are built on the premises that (1) individual students will vary and (2) if this var-

iance is not met with a flexible approach to programming by the school system, many students will fail.

Criterion-referenced tests (or any other set of tests) and diagnostic and placement documents illustrate that students do vary in their rates of learning, placement, styles, and levels of learning. Prescription systems are one means of insuring that teachers have the needed tools to do more than merely recognize that variance exists. They furnish the assistance to place students in textbooks, workbooks, worksheets, or audio-visuals at a point just beyond where the student has demonstrated prior success. They provide the capability of accurate and manageable prescription so that the teaching requirements of the diagnostic, placement, and prescriptive processes will not cause teachers to be in the untenable position of sacrificing student success in order to reduce an impossible management burden. Such an approach suggests that students' attitudes about themselves, their peer groups, and the school will, in no small measure, be affected by the degree of success achieved while in the school setting. In this instance, prescription systems are designed to help students maximize both their educational achievement and feelings of self-worth. Consequently, by recognizing and attending to individual student variances, prescription systems focus on the humanization of instruction.

(2) Prescription systems humanize programs by recognizing that there are alternative styles, modes, or patterns of student learning and a variety of different materials and experiences that teachers can use to assist students in skill attainment. Rather than being characterized as inflexible and unimaginative, prescription systems are designed to be open-ended, additive, varied, and inclusive. Any type of activity, experience, or material that conveys the intent of any skill being emphasized is an acceptable addition to a prescription system. In a similar manner, any methodological approach used by teachers that is effective in bringing about increased student achievement in and satisfaction from programs should be considered as a valuable technique for use with select students who are responsive to that methodology. Prescription systems are designed so that teachers and students may select or design any number of alternative paths to learning.

(3) Prescription systems humanize instructional programs by

acknowledging the need for a realistic balance among alternative methodological approaches in the classroom. Many school system programs are methodologically stereotypic: they promote one approach at the exclusion of all others thereby creating student frustration and failure. This is true, for example, in school systems that rely solely on either whole group instruction or individualized programs. Each approach has its place and when used at appropriate times they bear fruit, but there are also circumstances under which each is less than satisfactory.

For example, individualized instruction techniques are particularly effective for programs with a fairly heavy emphasis on cognitive skills. They offer the possibility of diagnosis, placement, and prescription for students at a variety of different points along established program foundations. They tender the opportunity for individuals and small groups of students to progress at varied learning rates, with differing styles, and at varied levels of skill abstraction. They are relatively unconcerned about delivering prescriptions to large groups of students or an entire class. In fact, it is unlikely that such prescription would occur to any degree. Such an approach is excellent for many programs but not for others. The application of an individualized instruction approach to some school system programs may alter their intended outcomes. As an example, a social studies program or a similarly oriented affective program intended to elicit general student discussion, value clarification, and judgment formation would be dramatically altered if used in conjunction with an individualized instruction approach. Small groups of students would rarely be working on the same skills, concepts, and processes, and there would be little basis for common discussion. Likewise, personal judgments, values, opinions, and attitudes could not be subjected to group discussion and examination, and the opportunity for affirmation of attitudes, opinions, judgments, and values held by students would be impossible. Thus, an impractical methodological procedure has distorted the focus of the program.

The exclusive use of whole group instruction has similar prescriptive and methodological strengths and weaknesses. Though whole group instruction does create an environment conducive to discussion, value clarification, and judgment formation, occasionally such instruction has adverse consequences for many students. Structuring whole group instruction for every program and course, though it will normally enhance *group* interaction, manifoldly increases the number of students who are misplaced. In many instances, whole group instruction and increased student interaction must give way to accurate diagnosis, placement, and prescription. To allow individual student failure at the expense of greater group interaction is an untenable rationalization about the intended results of a program. Certainly there are many programs whose content need not be subjected to the total class for discussion and validation (mathematics, reading, foreign language, vocational education, and so forth). In these programs, the use of whole group instruction to attain increased interaction is merely an instructional convenience that simplifies grouping and prescription activities for the teacher while sacrificing the learning success of many students.

Prescription systems are designed to permit a combination of both individualized and whole group instruction most appropriate for the students enrolled in a specific program and to enhance the accomplishment of desired program outcomes. This can be accomplished by constructing learning activities and materials sequenced to program foundation skills of graduated difficulty to enhance individualization—if that course of action is warranted and desired. In addition, the materials and learning activities can be written for each skill on different abstraction and readability levels to facilitate whole group instruction for students of varied abilities—if that is programmatically desirable. With such a prescription system, school systems can implement programs that can be either individualized or grouped as students' needs and program designs dictate. At the same time, the system will not sacrifice any of the successful features of existing school system methodological approaches.

(4) Prescription systems humanize programs through the inclusion of all skill classes in programs rather than extracting and treating some skill classes in special units, courses, or programs. Affective and psychomotor skills are identified parts of program foundations and are valued in the same manner as cognitive skills. Thus, students are exposed to fine and gross motor skills, opinion, judgment, value, career, and other personal decisions within the context of each program. Such an inclusion of seemingly more elusive affective and psychomotor skills insures that teachers will be as conscientious about exploring the purpose of their program, its career

potential, attitudes, values, and interests with students as they are in disseminating factual content.

The integration of all skill classes in prescription systems guarantees that issues that are important to students will be addressed by school system programs. It insures that some of the vital issues of education and life will be addressed. It militates against programs that are without feeling for or interest in the short or long term welfare of the student. It structures discussion on questions and problems that have more than one answer and, possibly, no universally correct answers. It offers some purposeful explanations of why students are in school, the consequences of limited schooling, and the need for formulating career plans.

For some inexplicable reason, much of the curricula of school systems has tended toward cognitive or factual information dissemination. The design may not be faulty but it is incomplete. Soundly designed prescription systems correct that omission.

Designing Effective Prescription Systems

Well designed prescription systems guide classroom teachers through the exacting process of locating appropriate learning activities and supportive materials for students who exhibit a variety of different placement positions. Prescription systems are logical extensions of previously designed program foundations, criterion-referenced tests, and placement documents.

The necessary components of a prescription system are (1) a prescription system organization, (2) instructional program foundations, (3) program skill cross-references, (4) instructional objectives, (5) performance criteria, (6) back-up test references and materials, (7) sample test items, (8) program content references, (9) supplementary and enrichment references and materials, and (10) procedures for prescription system usage.

Prescription System Organization. Prescription systems may contain hundreds of concisely stated skill units. Each unit focuses on teaching one or more basic skills, concepts, or processes in a program foundation and may contain scores of prescriptive references and supportive (worksheet and test) materials. The sheer volume of references and materials in a prescriptive system creates the need for a system organization that will aid teachers in locating desired units for skills under examination in as short a time as possible.

School systems have total latitude in selecting or designing an organization or format for their prescription systems, but some key features should be incorporated into it for ease of teacher access and usage. Among the salient features of a prescription system arrangement are (1) uniformity, (2) standard numbering system, (3) standard material divisions, and (4) pre-established content areas.

(1) Uniformity is basic to a prescription system. Each skill unit should be consistent in appearance and content areas treated, giving it congruence with every other unit in the system. Type, spacing, headings, punctuation, abbreviations, numbering, ordering, content areas treated, and content subdivisions should be standardized before the prescription system is written. If these precautionary steps are taken prior to designing the system, the final product will have the appearance of a professionally and thoughtfully constructed work, and classroom teachers using the system will not be distracted by organizational inconsistencies and omissions.

(2) A most critical element in system organization is the design of a standard numbering system for coding prescriptions. The standard numbering system is vital for locating the exact information desired by teachers for student prescription. Every page in the prescription system should contain a distinct number, identifying the subject or program, grade level, skill, and function of the page relative to the skill in question. The well constructed numbering system assists teachers in a multitude of different ways: locating skill units specified for placement on criterion-referenced tests or placement documents; locating a skill unit for supplementary instruction; requesting that specific worksheets, pretests, posttests, or other pieces of material be reproduced; locating skills that are cross-referenced to a specific skill; locating skill units that are cross-referenced to a skill or a unit; and locating test items that are used to assess mastery of a skill.

The numbering system needs to be flexible in its structure. For example, as a prescription system's contents are modified with teacher usage, and new materials are added, while faulty and outdated materials are extracted, it is a certainty that school systems will not want to renumber the entirety of their prescription system to accommodate those revisions. As a consequence, special care should be taken to insure that the numbering system is sufficiently sophisticated and flexible to accommodate the inclusions and deletions of new skill units, references, and materials to and from prescription systems without a loss of continuity, meaning, or time. (Such a numbering system is presented at the end of chapter 3.)

(3) Generally, prescription systems provide somewhat more than just prescriptive information to classroom teachers. Some systems furnish back-up testing systems; others provide supplemental references and materials; and some include broad supplemental reading or enrichment sections with a wealth of skill-based resource documents. Elaborate prescription systems contain all of these resources. For this reason, school systems will want to devote some time to identifying a number of standard material divisions into which their skill units will be divided.

The purpose of material divisions in skill units is merely to increase the facility with which desired materials can be located by teachers. When material divisions are established for a prescription system, they should occur consistently in each of the skill units, and their organization should be arranged in a logical sequence characteristic of the way in which teachers would normally use them with students (for example, prescriptive division, assessment division, supplementation division, resource and enrichment division). The contents of the material divisions in skill units are suggested by their names.

- The prescriptive division serves as a master plan, control sheet, or format page for each skill unit. It furnishes basic information on the prescriptive references, assessment instruments, supplemental materials, and enrichment resources that are available in the unit and in the school system. In addition, this division, which is always the first page of the skill unit, conveys information to the teacher in several pre-established content areas.
- The assessment division contains all back-up testing and answer keys pertinent to the skill under examination.
- The supplementation division includes student worksheets and answer keys that may be used to teach the skill and additional materials and learning activities contained in the school system's textbooks, workbooks, tapes, filmstrips, loops, and other formally adopted curricula.
- The resource and enrichment division contains resource documents that extend beyond the basic examination of the unit's skill and encourage further, more sophisticated study. (See figure 9)

Fig. 9
Material Divisions and Content Areas of a Skill Unit

DIVISION	CONTENT AREAS	CONTENTS
Prescriptive	Skill Unit Number	Format or Control Sheet
	Skill	
	Program Skill Cross-Reference	
	Instructional Objectives	
	Performance Criteria	
	Back-Up Test References	
	Sample Test Items	
	Program Content References	
	Supplemental References	
	Enrichment References	
Assessment		Documents:
		Back-Up Pretest
		Back-Up Posttest
		Answer Key
Supplementation		Basic Worksheet
		Basic Game
		Basic Activity
		Basic Description
		Basic Narrative
		Basic Exercise
		Basic Reading
		Basic Key
		Basic Guide
		Basic Puzzle
Resource &		Advanced Worksheet
Enrichment		Advanced Game
		Advanced Activity
		Advanced Description
		Advanced Narrative
		Advanced Exercise
		Advanced Reading
		Advanced Key
		Advanced Guide
		Advanced Puzzle

(4) Select pre-established content areas are contained in the prescription division of each skill unit. These guide teachers in using the skill units and, additionally, make them aware of all pertinent school system resources that can be used in the diagnosis, placement, prescription, assessment, and supplementation of students relative to the skill. Pre-established content areas most often treated in the prescriptive division of a skill unit are the following:

- The skill unit number
- The unit's skill
- Program skill cross-references
- Instructional objective(s)
- Performance criteria for the skill
- Back-up test references (Pretests and posttests)
- Sample test items
- Program content references
- Supplemental and enrichment references and materials (See figure 9)

Instructional Program Foundation. As in the case of the design of criterion-referenced tests and diagnostic and placement documents, the identification of program foundations is a requisite precursor to the development of prescription systems. Each skill, concept, and process, identified as critical to a school system's program and students' learning experiences becomes a part of the program foundation.

Once the program foundation skills are identified, sequenced in logical order, and affirmed for program inclusion, each skill is assigned a unique number depicting its subject or program, grade level, and position in relation to other skills at that grade level. The skill name and number are entered on the prescriptive division (control sheet or format page) of a skill unit. Teachers are then in a position to begin the process of constructing a detailed unit around the identified skill.

Program Skill Cross-References. The formal identification and sequencing of program foundations many times suggests to the teacher that skills have been arranged in a logical progression of increased difficulty, and the only dependency existing among them is between a specific skill and its preceding or following ones in the program foundation. If this in fact were true, in a sequence of skills—A, B, C, D, E—skill D would have a relationship with only skills C (one of dependency) and E (one of prerequisite importance) but have no relationship with Skills A or B. Such assumptions of dependency or lack of dependency are frequently in error. Program foundations may not always be sequenced according to skill difficulty, and a specific skill may not always be dependent upon only its preceding skill. More often than not, the mastery of a specific skill is dependent upon a multitude of other skills. Such a circumstance makes it vital that skill units have their program skills cross-referenced to permit teachers to establish the interdependency of a skill and its unit with other skills and units.

As a skill in a program foundation is examined, other skills with a direct relationship to it will need to be identified. Then, their names and numbers are entered into the cross-reference sections of skill units that rely upon them for mastery. Entries in the cross-reference section may appear as follows:

RD 151-050.00 Visual Discrimination, Colors
RD 151-065.00 Visual Discrimination, Shapes
RD 151-075.00 Visual Discrimination, b/d/p/q

Program skill cross-references can be used in conjunction with information reported on criterion-referenced tests and diagnostic inventories to minimize misplacement, inaccurate prescription, and student failure. For example, teachers can compare students' preplacement skill weaknesses identified on diagnostic inventories to skills identified in the cross-reference sections. If the skills match, it will be advisable for teachers to select the cross-referenced skill units (relating to preplacement skill weaknesses) and teach them prior to beginning prescription at students' placement positions suggested in diagnostic inventories. If this is not done, students may fail to acquire their first prescribed skill even though they are placed correctly. This point is illustrated below.

Diagnostic Inventory indicates placement at: SC 651-080.00
Diagnostic Inventory indicates that the student also
    has the following preplacement deficiencies: SC 651-065.00
                                           SC 651-050.00

Skill Unit SC 651-080.00 indicates that the following
    skills are of prerequisite importance to mastery of
    skill SC 651-080.00, and the likelihood of skill

acquisition is minimized if they are not acquired
prior to undertaking the skill: SC 651-075.00
                                                           SC 651-065.00
                                                           SC 651-050.00

Adjusted sequence of prescription is as follows: SC 651-050.00
                                                           SC 651-065.00
                                                           SC 651-080.00

It should be noted that the recommendation of an adjusted sequence of prescription (sequence for teaching skill units) does not invalidate or nullify the data reported on criterion-referenced tests and diagnostic inventories. The student's placement position was reported accurately above as SC 651-080.00, but preplacement skill weaknesses were also identified as having a direct bearing on the acquisition of that skill (as identified in the program skill cross-reference section of the skill). These preplacement skill deficiencies must be alleviated first. In another instance where preplacement skill deficiencies are identified that are not prerequisite to the placement skill, they will not be contained in the program skill cross-reference. As a consequence, prescription will begin at the placement point suggested on the student's diagnostic inventory.

Instructional Objectives. Each skill unit in a school system's prescription system contains a unique skill or combination of skills that teachers will present to students for acquisition. For each skill contained in the prescription system, one or more desired behaviors or outcomes are sought from students to illustrate that the skill prescribed and taught has been acquired. Because of the multiplicity of skills incorporated into a total prescription system, it is unlikely that teachers could be aware of and remember all of their desired student learning outcomes. For this reason, instructional objectives are written for each skill unit to govern the skill it contains. The instructional objective is inserted in the appropriate content area of the skill unit's prescriptive division.

The instructional objective is a simple, uncomplicated statement of the intent of a skill unit. It reinforces that the skill contained in the unit is the primary, significant issue to be conveyed, but its information extends beyond the mere restatement of the skill. It provides further information about "how" students will illustrate that they have acquired the skill and "how" teachers will assess whether or not acquisition has taken place.

Obviously skills can be taught in many different ways, and acquisition can be demonstrated and assessed in many different ways. Thus, instructional objectives merely suggest one or more ways for determining whether or not students have acquired the unit's skill. Teachers may modify instructional objectives to suit their particular mode of prescription and assessment as long as final student assessment indicates that the skill, concept, or process introduced has been acquired, and that students can subsequently demonstrate a facility for using the skill. This latter point reillustrates that the primary purpose of prescription is the student's acquisition and subsequent facility to use a skill, concept, or process in many different forms and settings. Thus, prescriptions should not be so rigidly governed by instructional objectives that teachers feel confined to a limited number of ways that they can introduce, prescribe, and assess a skill. Such a posture toward instructional objectives cultures an undesirable uniformity in approaching content and methodology and reduces teacher creativity and ingenuity in prescribing to students. This should be avoided at all costs.

Requisite characteristics of any instructional objective contained in skill units are (1) clarity in wording; (2) specificity of that which the student will be expected to perform in order to demonstrate skill acquisition; (3) uniformity in meaning for all potential readers; (4) a level of performance that students will be required to meet to demonstrate skill acquisition; (5) measurability; and (6) any conditions that are placed on the student during assessment that vary from conditions that were present during prescription. Many authors have treated these characteristics and provided detailed methodological procedures for writing instructional objectives. The reader may wish to examine the information written on this subject prior to undertaking the process of instructional objective writing.

Performance Criteria. Each instructional objective in each skill unit contains performance criteria or standards of performance for comparing students' assessed proficiencies against a desired level. Performance criteria are generally numerical figures (number of correct responses, percentage of correct responses, maximum time limit, and others). They are established to aid teachers in making reasonable determinations about (1) whether or not students have acquired a skill under study and (2) the likelihood that students will or will not fail on subsequent skills that are dependent upon the one completed.

There are no certain guidelines for determining the acceptable performance criteria for a specific skill. Some skills are more important than others, and some skills are more difficult than others. Consequently, performance standards may vary from one skill to the next, and curriculum designers can only gain confidence in their standards through usage, revision, and more usage. Nevertheless, performance criteria do play an important role in skill unit construction. Their presence serves as a reminder to teachers that performance below the criterion level is fraught with *potential* learning danger if students are permitted to undertake subsequent higher order skills before demonstrating proficiency on the skill under study. They also illustrate that the probability of future prescriptive failure is diminished if assessed performances on skills are greater than the suggested performance criteria.

Performance criteria are generally set within a 60 to 90 percent accuracy range on any specific skill, though standards vary considerably from school system to school system and from one skill to another. There are no data to indicate a "best" performance level, but, obviously, the higher the performance criterion is set the greater is the probability that any judgment made about a student's skill acquisition and readiness for subsequent prescription will be correct. Unfortunately, there is a point of diminishing return with continuing to set higher and higher performance criteria. That point is reached when students are scoring exceedingly well on assessment instruments (90 percent correct), which demonstrates a high level of skill mastery and, yet, are failing to reach arbitrarily high performance criteria (95 or 100 percent performance criteria). In instances such as this, performance criteria are not fulfilling their intended purpose, which suggests the need for supplementing or reinstructing students on unmastered skills. Rather, in this instance, the performance criteria are serving as unrealistic numerical barriers over which few students can climb. If students are being reinstructed in skills on which they have demonstrated 90 percent mastery, a serious error is being committed. Setting performance criteria at lofty positions or, also, at inordinately low levels (where virtually the most deficient students can meet the performance standard) misses the entire intent of performance criteria.

In the end, the ultimate performance indicators will be the teacher's judgment of a student's acquisition of a skill and his readiness for subsequent skill instruction. If the student fails to achieve the performance criterion on a skill, is allowed to progress to a subsequent dependent skill, and then fails, the teacher will need to reroute the student through the earlier skill anyway. Performance criteria merely aid in reducing the incidence of such trial and error failure by teachers.

Back-up Test References. Each skill unit contains references to back-up test materials that are available for assessing students both before and after prescription. The back-up test reference section of the skill unit specifies the standard number of any test inventories that are located in that unit's assessment division.

Back-up test materials supplement and strengthen the diagnostic capacity of the classroom teacher and reinforce or refute data obtained on school system criterion-referenced tests. Because school system criterion-referenced tests rarely use more than three to five items to assess each skill, classroom teachers have back-up tests available to reassess the accuracy of students' suggested placement positions. This can be done by administering a back-up test of eight to twenty items on the placement skill or any preceding or following skill where the teacher may have questions about the accuracy of criterion-referenced test data. In the event that back-up testing (pretesting) does indicate that students' knowledge of certain skills are inaccurately reflected on the criterion-referenced test, they can be retested using several single skill back-up tests until the correct placement position is located.

A second use of back-up test materials is to assess the extent of skill acquisition after formal prescription. Teachers may administer these single skill tests to determine whether or not students have acquired the skills under study. If the skills have not been acquired—as determined through a comparison of students' test scores and performance criteria—reintroduction or supplementation of the skills is in order.

Back-up test materials can also be employed to short-cut the learning process for some students. On occasion, a student may have knowledge of a skill prior to prescription. In this instance, the administration of a back-up test will affirm this knowledge and permit the student to by-pass formal prescription on the skill. This testing capability is most valuable in conserving both teacher and student time and eliminating the boredom that a capable student experiences when a school system is unable or unwilling to recognize prior knowledge of select skills and offer the possibility of advanced placement.

Sample Test Items. The prescriptive division of a skill unit normally contains illustrative sample test items that are representative of those found in back-up test materials and criterion-referenced tests. The purpose of such sample items is to provide the teacher with a brief view of the type of test questions that students will be required to answer to demonstrate skill mastery.

Including sample test items in skill units conserves teachers' time during review and selection of appropriate prescriptions for students. By examining these items, teachers can obtain an overview of the unit's back-up tests without actually studying them. Then, when an appropriate skill unit is located, the teacher may study the actual test documents in detail.

Program Content References. The most critical information section found in skill units is the program content reference. This section contains references to prescriptions that classroom teachers may use to alleviate student skill deficiencies identified on criterion-referenced tests.

Program content references are developed in conjunction with the identification of the instructional program foundation. As skills of instruction are identified, the locations of each skill in school system textual and supplementary materials are cited by author or publisher, title or reference, and page number. This documentation is entered into the program content reference section in the following form:

1. See Allyn and Bacon, *America,* pp.47–49.
2. Complete Scott Foresman, *Cultures in America,* pp.71–79.
3. Review American Britannica, *Tapes of Our Nation,* Tape 6.

Program content references increase in value as the numbers of options cited in skill units are increased. A well developed program content reference section may contain from ten to fifty suggested sources of prescription for a skill, and teachers may select any one or a combination of them to use with students for eliminating diagnosed deficiencies or establishing placement.

In addition to references to school system texts and supplementary materials, skill units also contain references to worksheet materials in the supplementation division of the unit itself. These materials will be noted in the program content reference section by their standard number, as follows:

1. Complete Worksheet AS 651-085.11
2. Work problems on Worksheet AS 651-080.13

In the main, these worksheet materials are considered back-up resources to a school system's basic textual and supplementary program. As a consequence, they are generally reserved for usage after the student has been placed in and failed with the school system's regularly adopted program. Nevertheless, their applicability for prescribing a skill contained in a unit is as appropriate as using basic school system textual materials.

Program content references should be viewed by school personnel as a resource base that can and should be continually revised and expanded to include greater numbers of references to which teachers can turn for assistance. Even changes in school system adoptions and the addition of new textual and supplementary holdings will not affect the appropriateness of existing program content references. The addition of new school system materials merely provides opportunities for enlarging the teacher's resource base for prescriptions. With usage and development, the program content reference section of each skill unit can become a virtual catalogue of resources to be used with students displaying different learning problems, varied learning styles, and receptivity to a variety of different methodological approaches and materials.

Supplementary and Enrichment References and Materials. Each skill unit contains an abundance of supplementary and enrichment references to school system adopted textbooks, workbooks, audio visuals, and other resource materials that may be used in the remediation of skill deficiencies or in broadening students' knowledge of a skill. In addition, the unit embodies worksheets, guides, passages, games, puzzles, or other written exercises that may be used by the teacher for supplemental and enrichment purposes. Supplementary and enrichment materials contained in school system materials or units are referenced in a manner identical to basic program content. The referencing, however, is located in the prescriptive division's section reserved for supplementary and enrichment materials. This section of the unit adds an additional dimension of resource assistance for classroom teachers. Its application is reserved for students who require detailed skill supplementation and, conversely, for those who are capable of more advanced and detailed examination of a skill under study.

Procedures for Prescription System Usage. School systems that have developed instructional program foundations, criterion-referenced tests, and diagnostic and placement documents will find an increased need for the development of prescription systems. As prescription systems are developed, written procedures on their usage will become more vital to insure proper application by classroom teachers.

Procedures for prescription system usage include an examination of the integration of diagnostic, placement, and prescriptive functions; the purpose of the prescriptive system; techniques of application; and general guidelines for minimizing teacher apprehensions in employing individualized instruction. A sample set of basic procedures for prescription system usage is documented below.

Procedures For Prescription System Usage

A GUIDE TO CLASSROOM TEACHERS

1. A prescription system is presented for your examination. The system is comprised of hundreds of self-contained skill units that are each written around one skill, concept, or process in our school system's program. The units are numbered and sequenced to coincide with the skills listed in the instructional program foundation. Each unit contains select materials and references to perform the following functions: pretesting, prescription, posttesting, supplementation, and enrichment or remediation.
2. The purpose of the prescription system is to aid you in locating a most desirable prescription for each of your students after they have been placed.
3. It is not mandatory that you use the prescription system or the prescriptions it suggests. However, it is a required function of the school system and its personnel—in the presence of documentation that will facilitate

accurate placement and prescription—to place and prescribe your students in a manner that will insure their success. Thus, your use or nonuse of the school system's prescription system does not minimize or eliminate the responsibility of the school system to insure that diagnostic, placement, and prescriptive activities are accurately performed. You may use any school system or personal resources to accomplish this requirement, but the requirement must be met.

4. The one mandatory element in the prescription system is the skill. The skills have been determined by staff members in our school system to be essential elements that students should be taught. After correct placement of the student, it is your responsibility to see that the student makes reasonable progress in skill acquisition from his point of placement. In this regard, the teacher is not responsible for insuring that a student is working on grade level skills or reaches grade level but, rather, that the student is placed correctly and proceeds to acquire skills from that point.

5. You have received copies of your students' criterion-referenced tests, diagnostic inventories, and class grouping reports. The students will have a documented placement position reported on their diagnostic inventory. Their placement position is identified by a number and the name of the skill. The number coincides with a skill in the instructional program foundation and a skill unit in the prescription system.

6. Review your diagnostic inventories and class grouping reports. Determine the approximate number of groups you will operate and the placement position for each group.

7. Select the appropriate skill unit for each group of students (the placement number will be the same as the skill unit number).

8. For each of your groups, examine the preplacement deficiencies of each student. Preplacement deficiencies are skill weaknesses identified on the diagnostic inventory that fall *before* the placement position.

9. Compare the preplacement deficiencies on the diagnostic inventory with skills cited in the program skill cross-reference section of the skill unit. These comparisons should be made for each student. If a student's preplacement deficiencies match—partially or totally—the skills cited in the program skill cross-reference section, place the student in the first deficient preplacement skill cited on both documents *rather than* at the placement position suggested on the diagnostic inventory. Select appropriate skill units for these students.

10. A placement position has now been determined and checked (or adjusted) for all students, and an appropriate skill unit has been selected for each group of students.

11. Administer a back-up test (pretest) to each of the groups.

12. Reread the skill, instructional objectives, performance criteria, and sample test item sections for each of the skill units selected for each group of students.

13. Have the students exchange their back-up tests and correct them. If the criterion-referenced test has correctly identified each student's placement position, the students should fail to achieve a test score at or above the performance criterion suggested in the skill unit.

14. Select a basic prescription for each group from the skill unit that is appropriate to their placement position. This will generally be an assignment into the school system's textual adoption. Assign the students to the prescription.

15. While the majority of the students are working on their prescription, continue to test students who demonstrated mastery on their placement skill. Merely select a back-up test (pretest) from the skill unit of the next advanced skill and administer it. Continue this procedure until the student fails to achieve the performance criterion. Then, select an appropriate prescription from that skill unit and assign it to the student.

16. Meet with each of the groups for discussion, monitoring, and assessment purposes.

17. As groups of students complete prescriptive activities, administer a back-up test (posttest) to affirm or refute skill mastery. On many occasions, back-up testing is not necessary if the students have just completed independent activities, and the results of those activities indicate skill mastery.

18. If the students demonstrate skill acquisition by attaining the desired performance criterion or you have confidence in the students' work, the students will be prescribed learning activities for the subsequent skill and skill unit in the program foundation.

19. Students who do not demonstrate skill mastery may be supplemented by selecting an alternative program prescription, supplemental materials from the unit's supplementation division, or remedial materials from the unit's resource and enrichment division. Such supplementation should be followed up with a formal back-up testing (posttest) to insure skill acquisition.

20. Early in this process you will want to meet with other teachers (lower level, higher level, and same level) in the building to examine procedures for student grouping and establishing the number, placement positions, and organization of groups. You may wish to consider cross-grade and cross-unit grouping to increase the effectiveness, efficiency, and manageability of prescription.

21. You should be aware that the prescriptive system is not a perfect product and will be revised annually. You are encouraged to add materials to it, identify deficiencies, and increase the number of references. Sometime in the early spring requests will be made for criticisms of and suggestions for the improvement of the system and its contents. Your suggestions, criticisms, deletions, insertions, and materials will be valued. They will be screened by a team of teachers and assessed for their

appropriateness in causing additions, deletions, and modifications of the system.

Design Work for the Teacher

Developing a prescription system (especially if you are doing it alone) is unquestionably the most time consuming task in the diagnostic, placement, and prescriptive process. Even so, a miniaturized prescription system can be constructed fairly quickly using work that has already been completed in the process of stating the program foundation and gathering information required for diagnosis and placement.

The beginning point in prescription system development is to establish the content that will be contained in the prescriptive division or first page of each of your skill units. The prescriptive division is the control page of each unit, and customarily, it contains information about the skill unit number (or skill number), the skill name, program skill cross-references, instructional objectives, performance criteria, back-up test references, sample test items, program content references, supplemental references, and enrichment references. If you decide to include all of these types of information in your skill units, remember that you need not complete them all at once. Rather, certain parts of this division can be completed immediately and others when time is available or the need is apparent. Now, type out a prescriptive division outline and reproduce fifty or so copies. Figure 10 is an example of the outline. You may find it beneficial to leave fairly large areas in several of the sections of the prescriptive division to allow plenty of room for information that will be entered. In fact, as the prescriptive division outline is typed, you will find it valuable to spread the outline over two, full pages.

With several blank prescriptive division outlines in hand, you will note that for any given skill, concept, or process, quite a bit of information has already been developed. For example, you previously identified the skill and ascribed to it a skill (or skill unit) number. Program skill cross-references were completed, test items developed, and several program content references written. Thus, five of the nine information categories have already been completed.

The above information should be written into the blank prescrip-

Fig. 10
Prescriptive Division of Skill Unit

Skill Unit Number:

Skill:

Program Skill Cross-References:

Instructional Objectives:

Performance Criteria:
Back-Up Test References:

Sample Test Items:

Program Content References:

Supplemental and Enrichment References:

tive division outlines for each skill, concept, or process you have
identified. This is a simple copying job from documents previously
developed. You now have a series of partially developed skill units
in your prescription system.

The content areas of the prescriptive division that remain unde-
veloped at this stage of writing are the instructional objectives, performance criteria for the skill, back-up test references, and supplemental and enrichment references and materials. The instructional
objectives should be written next.

Prior to writing instructional objectives, you may want to review
some of the appropriate books listed in the bibliography. If time does
not permit this, it is suggested that you again turn to the content of
the skill (textbooks, workbooks, materials, and media used to teach
the skills in question) about which you are writing one or more

instructional objectives and study the types of learning experiences to which you will expose your students in teaching them the skill. Then, ask yourself the following questions:

- How do I expect the students to demonstrate mastery on this skill?
- What will I ask students to perform to show their mastery?
- Are there any special conditions about the way I will ask students to perform the skill?
- How well must students perform to cause me to be confident that they have mastered a skill?

With these questions in mind, you will answer them by merely writing an objective statement. This will be placed in the skill unit's prescriptive division. For example, in a physical education class, an objective may be written as follows:

The student will perform six exercises, including push-ups, sit-ups, rope climbing, deep knee-bends, chin-ups, and the side-straddle hop. He will begin the exercises after a brief five minute warm up period. He will complete a minimum of ten push-ups, 25 sit-ups, a climb of twenty feet in ten seconds, 30 deep knee-bends, six chin-ups, and 30 side-straddle hops.

One or more objective statements are written for each skill in the program foundation as a guide for carrying out teaching and testing activities. These are inserted in the instructional objective section of the prescriptive division (first page) of the skill unit.

Objectives need not be written any more elaborately than the statement above, but make a conscientious effort to be clear and concise in defining exactly what students will be asked to perform in order to demonstrate skill mastery. Later, when you are assessing your students, the objectives will serve as a benchmark for testing, and you will want to be sure that the student outcomes desired from learning activities are the same as those emphasized and encouraged in teaching and testing students.

After you have written instructional objectives for each skill and skill unit, you will also have delineated performance criteria for each. In the example above, it was specified that the students "will complete a minimum of ten push-ups, 25 sit-ups, a climb of twenty feet in ten seconds, 30 deep knee-bends, six chin-ups, and 30 side-straddle hops." This is the objective's performance criterion, and it should be copied on the prescriptive division in the space for performance criteria. The special citation of the performance criterion in a content area by itself does nothing more than isolate this information for ease of location. Further, it reemphasizes that you should be certain to state a performance criterion for each skill. If writing the performance criterion twice in the skill unit seems unnecessarily repetitious, forego writing it in the instructional objective and merely cite it in the space allotted for the performance criterion.

The two remaining content areas in the prescriptive division are the back-up test references and the supplemental and enrichment references. These content areas will contain standard numbers for tests and answer keys you may include in the assessment division of the skill unit and worksheets, guides, games, activities, puzzles, narratives, keys, and other materials included in the supplementation, resource, and enrichment divisions of the skill unit—*if* you decide to develop or appropriate such materials. Presuming you decide to develop a few back-up tests and several worksheets for each skill unit, you will assign standard numbers to each document and cite these numbers in the appropriate content areas, as is done below for a shorthand skill unit:

Back-up Test References: SH 701-005.01 (Pretest)
                           SH 701-005.03 (1st Posttest)
                           SH 701-005.05 (2nd Posttest)
Supplemental and Enrichment References: SH 701-005.11
                                          SH 701-005.12
                                          SH 701-005.13
                                          SH 701-005.14

Again, the standard number codes above are derived from the numbering system suggested at the end of chapter 3.

For each standard number code listed in the back-up test reference section and the supplemental and enrichment references' section of the prescriptive division, there should be corresponding documents (with the same number) that are found in the assessment and supplementation, resource, and enrichment divisions of the skill unit.

Having completed the developmental activities suggested above for each skill in your program foundation, you now have a set of usable, skeletal skill units that forms a prescription system for your course. From this point, any additional efforts you undertake will increase the sophistication and utility of your system. It is suggested that you continue to expand the number of program content references to school system textbooks, workbooks, materials, and media. Then, develop additional back-up tests and answer keys for them. As time permits, develop additional supplemental, resource, and enrichment documents and answer keys. The developmental process can be endless, and exposure to new materials, experience in material usage, and information and material exchanges with colleagues will increase the quality and quantity of resources you can acquire. However, if you are developing a prescription system by yourself, it can and should be a multiyear project that conforms to your own schedule and goals.

With the basic design of the skill units in a prescription system completed, you will want to spend some time reviewing procedures for using the prescription system. Review the procedures detailed earlier in this chapter; if they are not satisfactory for your particular circumstances, design some that will reflect the basic operations you intend to carry out in implementing a prescription system. They will help govern your approach to diagnosis, placement, and prescription: a criterion-referenced approach.

Documents

Two skill unit documents appear on the following pages to illustrate the content and organization of information in a prescription system.

Document 9 is a skill unit for second grade mathematics. Document 10 is a skill unit for seventh grade reading. The purpose in selecting these units for illustration is the high frequency with which students fail these programs. Skill units in other programs at the elementary or secondary level could be as easily illustrated. Likewise, affective and psychomotor skill units are as easily constructed as are cognitive ones. As long as school personnel begin the process with the identification of program foundations, the development of a prescription system is a matter of acquiring and delineating appropriate materials to convey each skill, whether cognitive, affective, or psychomotor, according to the suggested format. All of the philosophical and procedural actions taken after program foundation specification—design, development, implementation, and assessment of instructional units—remain unaltered.

Document 9
A Skill Unit for Second Grade Mathematics

SKILL UNIT NUMBER: MA 201-065.00

SKILL: Addition and subtraction combinations through 10.

PROGRAM SKILL CROSS-REFERENCES:

    MA 201-045.00 Addition Concepts, Sums of 10 or Less

    MA 201-050.00 Subtraction Concepts, Take Away
                  and Comparison of Sets

    MA 201-055.00 Inverse Relationship Between Addition
                  and Subtraction

    MA 201-060.00 Cumulative Property in Addition

INSTRUCTIONAL OBJECTIVES: To reinforce skills in working with combinations of ten or less, to introduce the use of the addition table, and to provide additional practice in working with word problems, the student will compute accurately 18 out of 20 problems using either the addition table or the number line.

BACK-UP TEST REFERENCES: MA 201-065.01
                           MA 201-065.03
                           MA 201-065.05

SAMPLE TEST ITEMS: 1)

+	1	2	3	4
1	2	3	4	5
2	3	4	5	6

2)   4
      +3

3) 6 + 3 =

4) 9 - 4 =

5) 8
     -2

PROGRAM CONTENT REFERENCES:

1. Do p. 53, AW2. Check.

2. Teacher directed, AW2, p. 54.

3. Do AW2, Duplicator Master, p. 18, teacher directed. Group check.

4. MA 201-065.11. Check.

5. Teacher directed, AW2, pp. 55, 67, and 69.

6. Do AW2, p. 56. Check.

7. Do AW2, pp. 57-58. Check.

8. Do AW2, pp. 59-60. Check.

9. Do AW2, pp. 61-62. Check.

10. Do AW2, Duplicator Master, p. 19. Check.

11. Do AW2, pp. 63-64. Check.

12. Do AW2, Duplicator Master, pp. 20-21. Check.

13. Do AW2, pp. 68 and 70. Check.

14. Do AW2, Duplicator Master, p. 22. Check.

15. Do AW2, Review Tests, Test 4, pp. 9 and 10. Check.

16. Post-Test MA 201-065.03. Teacher check.

SUPPLEMENTAL AND ENRICHMENT REFERENCES:

1. Do MA 201-065.13. Check.

2. Do Possible Activity, "Combo 1", AW2, teacher's manual, p. 87. Check.

3. Do AW2, Follow-up, teacher's manual, p. 89. Check.

4. Do AW2, Possible Activity, teacher's manual, pp. 90-91. Check.

5. Do MA 201-065.15. Check.

6. Do MA 201-065.17. Check.

7. Do MA 201-065.19. Check.

8. Do AW2, pp. 65-66. Check.

9. Do MA 201-065.21. Check.

10. Do MA 201-065.23. Check.

11. Post-Test MA 201-060.05. Teacher Check.

1.

+	0	1	2	3	4	5	6	7	8	9
0							6			
1				4						
2							8			
3										
4										
5			7							
6					10					
7										
8		9								
9										

18 out of 20

Complete the table.

Name _____

Score _____

Use the table to find the sums.

2. 8 + 2 = ___   4. 7 + 2 = ___

3. 4 + 4 = ___   5. 6 + 3 = ___

                       6. 4 + 6 = ___

7. 3   8. 9   9. 5   10. 5
   +5   +1   +4   +5
   ──   ──   ──   ──

11. Mother made a cake. She put
    2 cups of flour in the bowl.
    Sue put 1 more cup of flour
    into the bowl. How many cups
    of flour did they use alto-
    gether? ___ O ___ = ___

12. Dave had 5 bugs. He gave Jim
    2 of his bugs. How many did
    he have left? ___ O ___ = ___

Study the number line. Then solve the equation.

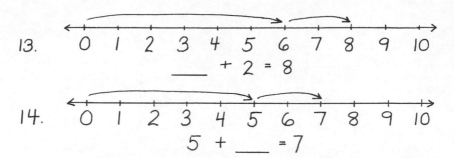

13. ___ + 2 = 8

14. 5 + ___ = 7

Solve the equations.

15. 5 + ___ = 9

16. ___ + 3 = 10

Solve the equations.

17. ___ + 5 = 9
    9 − 5 = ___

18. ___ + 9 = 9
    9 − 9 = ___

19. 9
    −4

20. 7
    −5

+	0	1	2	3	4	5	6	7	8	9
0	0	1	2	3	4	5	6	7	8	9
1	1	2	3	4	5	6	7	8	9	10
2	2	3	4	5	6	7	8	9	10	
3	3	4	5	6	7	8	9	10		
4	4	5	6	7	8	9	10			
5	5	6	7	8	9	10				
6	6	7	8	9	10					
7	7	8	9	10						
8	8	9	10							
9	9	10								

2) 10

3) 8

4) 9

5) 9

6) 10

7) 8

8) 10

9) 9

10) 10

11) 2 + 1 = 3

12) 5 - 2 = 3

13) 6

14) 2

15) 4

16) 7

17) 4
    4

18) 0
    0

19) 5

20) 2

SKILL UNIT NUMBER: MA 201-065.00
POST-TEST: MA 201-065.03

1.

+	0	1	2	3	4	5	6	7	8	9
0							6			
1				4						
2							8			
3										
4										
5			7							
6				10						
7										
8		9								
9										

Complete the table.

Name _____

Score _____

Find the sums.

2. 5 + 4 = ☐   4. 7 + 2 = ☐

3. 9 + 1 = ☐   5. 5 + 0 = ☐

Solve the equations.

6. ooooooooo   7. ▵ ▵ ▵ ▵▵▵▵ ▵
    4 + ☐ = 9   ☐ + 3 = 7

8. ‖‖‖‖‖‖‖   9. ▵ ▵▵▵ ▵ ▵ ▵ ▵ ▵▵
    7 + ☐ = 8   ☐ + 4 = 10

Study the number line. Then solve the equation.

10.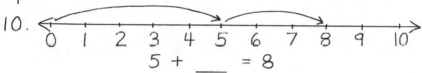

5 + ___ = 8

11.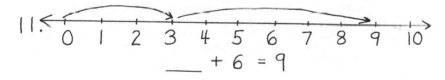

___ + 6 = 9

12. $\boxed{} + 3 = 8 \longrightarrow 8 - 3 = \boxed{}$

13. $\boxed{} + 6 = 9 \longrightarrow 9 - 6 = \boxed{}$

Solve.

14.   8   15.   10   16.   9
      -3   -4   -2

Put + or - in each ____.

17.   5 ___ 2 = 7

18.   9 ___ 3 = 6

19.   Charles and Steve are planting a garden. Charles has 8 seeds. He gives Steve 5. How many does he have left? _____

Steve found 4 worms and Charles found 3. How many did they find in all? _____

Steve had 7 plants. He gave
Charles 2. How many did he
have left? _____

20. Sally and Jane went to a farm.
Sally saw 8 ducks and Jane
saw 2. How many more did
Sally see than Jane? _____

Sally had 4 rides on the horse.
Jane had 6 rides. How many
rides did they have in all?

_____

+	0	1	2	3	4	5	6	7	8	9
0	0	1	2	3	4	5	6	7	8	9
1	1	2	3	4	5	6	7	8	9	10
2	2	3	4	5	6	7	8	9	10	
3	3	4	5	6	7	8	9	10		
4	4	5	6	7	8	9	10			
5	5	6	7	8	9	10				
6	6	7	8	9	10					
7	7	8	9	10						
8	8	9	10							
9	9	10								

2) 9
3) 10
4) 9
5) 5
6) 5
7) 4
8) 1
9) 6
10) 3
11) 3

12) 5 5
13) 3 3
14) 5
15) 6
16) 7
17) +
18) −

19) 8   4   7
    −5   +3   −2
    ─── ─── ───
     3   7   5

20) 8   4
    −2   +6
    ─── ───
     6   10

SKILL UNIT NUMBER: MA 201-065.00
POST-TEST: MA 201-065.05

Name _____

18 out of 20   Score _____

1. Complete the table.

+	0	1	2	3	4
0					
1					
2					
3					
4					

Find the sums.

2. 4   3. 3   4. 4   5. 3   6. 0
   +5   +4   +2   +5   +7

7. 2 + 5 = ☐   8. 2 + 2 = ☐

Find the missing addend.

9. 9   10. 10   11. 8   12. 6   13. 5
   -6   -6   -7   -4   -3

14. 9 - 5 = ☐   15. 8 - 7 = ☐

Find the answers on the number line.

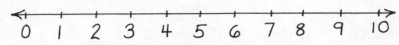

16. $\boxed{} + 2 = 6$ 18. $5 + 2 = \boxed{}$

17. $6 + \boxed{} = 8$ 19. $\boxed{} + 7 = 9$

2.   Sue and Jane were making cup-
     cakes. Sue made 4 cupcakes.
     Jane made 5. How many did they
     make together? _____

SKILL UNIT NUMBER: MA 201–065.00
POST–TEST KEY: MA 201–065.06

18 out of 20

1) Complete the table

+	0	1	2	3	4
0	0	1	2	3	4
1	1	2	3	4	5
2	2	3	4	5	6
3	3	4	5	6	7
4	4	5	6	7	8

2) 9
3) 7
4) 6
5) 8
6) 7
7) 7
8) 4
9) 3
10) 4
11) 1
12) 2
13) 2
14) 4
15) 1
16) 4
17) 2
18) 7
19) 2
20) 4 + 5 = 9

DOCUMENT 9

SKILL UNIT NUMBER: MA 201-065.00
WORKSHEET: MA 201-065.11

1.

+	0	1	2	3	4	5	6	7	8	9
0							6			
1				4						
2							8			
3										
4										
5			7							
6				10						
7										
8		9								
9										

Complete the table.

Name _____

Use the table to solve the equations.

2.   9
    +0

3.   3
    +3

4.   4
    +3

5.   8
    +2

6.   7
    +2

7.   6
    +3

8.   7
    +3

9.   1
    +1

10.   2
    +2

11.   2
    +3

12.   3
    +1

13.   1
    +9

14.   6
    +2

15.   9
    +1

16.   2
    +5

17.   4
    +5

18.   0
    +5

19.   4
    +6

20.   3
    +6

21.   2
    +7

22.   3
    +7

23.   3
    +5

24.   1
    +8

+	0	1	2	3	4	5	6	7	8	9
0	0	1	2	3	4	5	6	7	8	9
1	1	2	3	4	5	6	7	8	9	10
2	2	3	4	5	6	7	8	9	10	
3	3	4	5	6	7	8	9	10		
4	4	5	6	7	8	9	10			
5	5	6	7	8	9	10				
6	6	7	8	9	10					
7	7	8	9	10						
8	8	9	10							
9	9	10								

2)	9	13)	10	24)	9
3)	6	14)	8		
4)	7	15)	10		
5)	10	16)	7		
6)	9	17)	9		
7)	9	18)	5		
8)	10	19)	10		
9)	10	20)	9		
10)	4	21)	9		
11)	5	22)	10		
12)	4	23)	8		

Name _____

Score _____

1.
```
  +3
  ———
   8
```

2. 7
```
  +
  ——
  10
```

3. 4
```
  +
  ——
  7
```

4.
```
  +4
  ——
   9
```

5.
```
  +6
  ——
   8
```

6. 3
```
  +
  ——
  9
```

7. 6
```
  +
  ——
  10
```

8. 2
```
  +
  ——
  10
```

9. 8
```
  +
  ——
  10
```

10. 2
```
  +
  ——
  7
```

11.
```
  +8
  ——
   9
```

12.
```
  +4
  ——
   8
```

13. 4
```
  +
  ——
  6
```

14. 5
```
  +
  ——
  7
```

15.
```
  +5
  ——
  10
```

16.
```
  +2
  ——
   9
```

Find the missing numbers.

1) 5	5) 2	9) 2	13) 2
2) 3	6) 6	10) 5	14) 2
3) 3	7) 4	11) 1	15) 5
4) 5	8) 8	12) 4	16) 7

Name _____

Score _____

Find the missing addend.

1. ☐ + 5 = 8   2. ☐ + 4 = 8

3. ☐ + 4 = 7   4. ☐ + 2 = 7

5. ☐ + 5 = 10

6. ☐ + 4 = 6   7. ☐ + 4 = 10

8. ☐ + 3 = 5   9. ☐ + 3 = 10

10. ☐ + 4 = 9

11. ☐ + 2 = 10   12. ☐ + 5 = 7

13. ☐ + 2 = 6   14. ☐ + 3 = 10

15. ☐ + 2 = 9

16. ☐ + 3 = 6   17. ☐ + 2 = 8

18. ☐ + 5 = 7   19. ☐ + 6 = 10

20. ☐ + 3 = 7

SKILL UNIT NUMBER: MA 201-065.00
WORKSHEET KEY: MA 201-065.16

1) 3	6) 2	11) 8	16) 3
2) 4	7) 6	12) 2	17) 6
3) 3	8) 2	13) 4	18) 2
4) 5	9) 7	14) 7	19) 4
5) 5	10) 5	15) 7	20) 4

Name _____

Score _____

Find the patterns. Then write the correct numerals in the blanks.

1. Since 49 + 35 = 84, we know that 84 - 35 = ____ .

2. Since 17 + 48 = 65, we know that 65 - 48 = ____ .

3. Since 38 + 61 = 99, we know that 99 - 61 = ____ .

4. Since 27 + 54 = 81, we know that 81 - 54 = ____ .

5. Since 46 + 29 = 75, we know that 75 - ____ = 46.

6. Since 53 + 14 = 67, we know that 67 - ____ = 53.

7. Since 70 + 37 = 107, we know that 107 - ____ = 70.

8. Since 85 + 11 = 96, we know that 96 - ____ = 85.

SKILL UNIT NUMBER: MA 201-065.00
WORKSHEET KEY: MA 201-065.18

1) 49

2) 17

3) 38

4) 27

5) 29

6) 14

7) 37

8) 11

Write the correct numerals in the answer boxes. Then write the corresponding letters in the message boxes.

CODE
0 C
1 A
2 N
3 F
4 V
5 G
6 S
7 H
8 E
9 U

1) 3
   +4

2) 8
   −7

3) 9
   −5

4) 5
   +3

5) 3
   +0

6) 7
   +2

7) 8
   −6

Answer ☐ ☐ ☐ ☐ ☐ ☐ ☐

Message ☐ ☐ ☐ ☐ ☐ ☐ ☐

Name _____
Score _____

Answer   1) _7_   2) _1_   3) _4_   4) _8_   5) _3_   6) _9_   7) _2_

Message   H   A   V   E   F   U   N

SKILL UNIT NUMBER: MA 201-065.00
WORKSHEET: MA 201-065.21

Name _____
Score _____

Solve the equations.

1. 3 + 5 = ☐
    3 + ___ = 8
    ___ + 5 = 8

2. 2 + 8 = ☐
    2 + ___ = 10
    ___ + 8 = 10

3. 9 + 1 = ☐
    ___ + 1 = 10
    9 + ___ = 10

4. 7 + 3 = ☐
    7 + ___ = 10
    ___ + 3 = 10

5. 6 + 3 = ☐
    6 + ___ = 9
    ___ + 3 = 9

6. 2 + 7 = ☐
    ___ + 7 = 9
    2 + ___ = 9

7. 4 + 5 = ☐
    ___ + 5 = 9
    4 + ___ = 9

8. 4 + 6 = ☐
    4 + ___ = 10
    ___ + 6 = 10

9. $6 + 2 = \boxed{}$

$6 + \underline{} = 8$

$\underline{} + 2 = 8$

What other equations do you know?

SKILL UNIT NUMBER: MA 201-065.00
WORKSHEET KEY: MA 201-065.22

1)	8	4)	10	7)	9
	5		3		4
	3		7		5

2)	10	5)	9	8)	10
	8		3		6
	2		6		4

3)	10	6)	9	9)	8
	9		2		2
	1		7		6

SKILL UNIT NUMBER: MA 201-065.00
WORKSHEET: MA 201-065.23

Name _____

Score _____

Solve.

1. 4 + 5 = ☐	7. 10 - 7 = ☐
2. 7 - 4 = ☐	8. 3 + 5 = ☐
3. 5 + 2 = ☐	9. 9 - 2 = ☐
4. 10 - 8 = ☐	10. 4 + 2 = ☐
5. 3 + 3 = ☐	11. 9 - 5 = ☐
6. 8 - 6 = ☐	12. 1 + 9 = ☐

1.   8
   -3
	2. 7
	   +2
		3. 5
		   -1
			4. 4
			   +4

5.   3
   +2
	6. 6
	   -2
		7. 9
		   -2
			8. 1
			   +7

9.   10   10.   6   11.   2   12.   10
     -4   +3   +6   -5

Practice more equations here.

SKILL UNIT NUMBER: MA 201-065.00
WORKSHEET KEY: MA 201-065.24

1) 9   7) 3   1) 5   7) 7

2) 3   8) 8   2) 9   8) 8

3) 7   9) 7   3) 4   9) 6

4) 2   10) 6   4) 8   10) 9

5) 6   11) 4   5) 5   11) 8

6) 2   12) 10   6) 4   12) 5

Document 10
A Skill Unit for Seventh Grade Reading

SKILL UNIT NUMBER:　RD 451-010.00

SKILL:　Secondary Reading:　Alphabet and Alphabetical Order

PROGRAM SKILL CROSS-REFERENCES:　None

INSTRUCTIONAL OBJECTIVES:　In order to demonstrate his knowledge of the alphabet, the student will write the capital and lower case letters both from memory in sequence and from oral dictation with 80% accuracy.

BACK-UP TEST REFERENCES:　RD 451-010.01
RD 451-010.03
RD 451-010.05

SAMPLE TEST ITEMS:　I.　Fill in the blank spaces with the correct letters which come directly before and directly after the letters listed below.

　　　　　　 e 　　　 f 　　　 g

II. The teacher will say the letter "A" and the student will write the letter a or A.

PROGRAM CONTENT REFERENCES:

1.　Do Worksheet:　RD 451-010.11.　Teacher Directed.

2.　Do Worksheet:　RD 451-010.13.　Teacher Directed.

3.　Do Worksheet:　RD 451-010.15.　Teacher Directed.

4.　Do Worksheet:　RD 451-010.17.　Teacher Directed.

5.　Do Worksheet:　RD 451-010.19.　Teacher Directed.

6.　Do Worksheet:　RD 451-010.21.　Teacher Directed.

7.　Do Post Test:　RD 451-010.03.　Teacher Directed.

SUPPLEMENTAL AND ENRICHMENT REFERENCES:

1.　Do Activity:　RD 451-010.23.

2.　Do Activity:　RD 451-010.25.

3.　Do Post Test:　RD 451-010.05.　Teacher Directed.

SKILL UNIT NUMBER: RD 451-010.00
PRE-TEST: RD 451-010.01

I. Some of the letters in the alphabet have been left out. Fill in
    the blank spaces with the proper letter to make the alphabet
    correct.

    A ___ C ___ E ___ G ___ I ___ K ___ M ___ O ___ Q ___ S ___ U ___

    W ___ Y ___.

II. Listen carefully. The teacher will name one letter in each of the
    boxes. Circle the letter you hear.

1.	2.	3.	4.	5.	6.	7.
c r e a	z s x r	w n m v	x u y v	b d c a	r t s u	f h g a
8.	9.	10.	11.	12.	13.	14.
k n r t	n a p t	n a m r	w x y z	s d t v	k n j u	e i o u
15.	16.	17.	18.	19.	20.	21.
q s t a	a y s v	d c g a	n l y f	z o n t	v e p u	h g i j
22.	23.	24.	25.	26.		
a w x e	o i e u	m t u s	g h f o	m o p n		

SKILL UNIT NUMBER: RD 451-010.00
POST-TEST KEY: RD 451-010.02

I. A <u>B</u> C <u>D</u> E <u>F</u> G <u>H</u> I <u>J</u> K <u>L</u> M <u>N</u>

    O <u>P</u> Q <u>R</u> S <u>T</u> U <u>V</u> W <u>X</u> Y <u>Z</u>.

II. 1. e
   2. x
   3. v
   4. u
   5. b
   6. r
   7. h
   8. k
   9. a
  10. m
  11. z
  12. d
  13. j

14. o
15. q
16. y
17. c
18. 1
19. t
20. p
21. g
22. w
23. 1
24. s
25. f
26. n

SKILL UNIT NUMBER: RD 451-010.00
POST-TEST: RD 451-010.03

I. Fill in the blank spaces with the correct letters which come
    directly before and directly after the letters listed below.

    1. ___ b ___   6. ___ l ___

    2. ___ p ___   7. ___ q ___

    3. ___ x ___   8. ___ t ___

    4. ___ e ___   9. ___ v ___

    5. ___ i ___   10. ___ d ___

II. Write the alphabet using capital letters.

III. Write the alphabet using lower case letters.

IV. As the teacher says the letter, the student will write the
     letter.

    1. ___   8. ___   15. ___   22. ___

    2. ___   9. ___   16. ___   23. ___

    3. ___   10. ___   17. ___   24. ___

    4. ___   11. ___   18. ___   25. ___

    5. ___   12. ___   19. ___   26. ___

    6. ___   13. ___   20. ___

    7. ___   14. ___   21. ___

SKILL UNIT NUMBER: RD 451–010.00
POST-TEST KEY: RD 451–010.04

I. 1. a, c   6. k, m
    2. o, q   7. p, r
    3. w, y   8. s, u
    4. d, f   9. u, w
    5. h, j   10. c, e

II. A B C D E F G H I J K L M N O P Q R S T U V W X Y Z

III. a b c d e f g h i j k l m n o p q r s t u v w x y z

IV. 1. n   14. j
     2. f   15. d
     3. s   16. z
     4. i   17. m
     5. w   18. a
     6. g   19. k
     7. p   20. h
     8. t   21. r
     9. l   22. b
    10. c   23. u
    11. y   24. v
    12. q   25. x
    13. o   26. e

SKILL UNIT NUMBER: RD 451-010.00
POST-TEST: RD 451-010.05

I.   Write the alphabet using capital letters.

II. Write the alphabet using lower case letters.

III. Using the order of the alphabet, fill in the blank spaces
     with the correct letters which come directly before and
     directly after the letters listed below.

     1. ____ D ____   6. ____ C ____

     2. ____ K ____   7. ____ M ____

     3. ____ O ____   8. ____ Q ____

     4. ____ P ____   9. ____ X ____

     5. ____ V ____   10. ____ R ____

IV. As the teacher says the letter, the student will write
     the letter.

     1. ____   8. ____   15. ____   22. ____

     2. ____   9. ____   16. ____   23. ____

     3. ____   10. ____   17. ____   24. ____

     4. ____   11. ____   18. ____   25. ____

     5. ____   12. ____   19. ____   26. ____

     6. ____   13. ____   20. ____

     7. ____   14. ____   21. ____

SKILL UNIT NUMBER: RD 451–010.00
POST-TEST KEY: RD 451–010.06

I.   A B C D E F G H I J K L M N O P Q R S T U V W X Y Z

II. a b c d e f g h i j k l m n o p q r s t u v w x y z

III.   1. c, e   6. b, d
       2. j, l   7. l, n
       3. n, p   8. p, r
       4. o, q   9. w, y
       5. u, w   10. p, r

IV.   1. m   14. i
       2. z   15. s
       3. d   16. f
       4. j   17. n
       5. o   18. e
       6. q   19. x
       7. y   20. v
       8. c   21. u
       9. l   22. b
      10. t   23. r
      11. p   24. h
      12. g   25. k
      13. w   26. a

SKILL UNIT NUMBER: RD 451-010.00
WORKSHEET: RD 451-010.11

I. Copy each capital letter of the alphabet in the space provided below.

A	B	C	D	E	F	G	H	I	J	K	L	M
__	__	__	__	__	__	__	__	__	__	__	__	__
N	O	P	Q	R	S	T	U	V	W	X	Y	Z
__	__	__	__	__	__	__	__	__	__	__	__	__

II. Copy each lower case letter of the alphabet in the space provided below.

a	b	c	d	e	f	g	h	i	j	k	l	m
__	__	__	__	__	__	__	__	__	__	__	__	__
n	o	p	q	r	s	t	u	v	w	x	y	z
__	__	__	__	__	__	__	__	__	__	__	__	__

III. Write the letter of the alphabet which comes between the two letters already given.

1. a ___ c   6. w ___ y   11. U ___ W

2. e ___ g   7. n ___ p   12. t ___ v

3. c ___ e   8. F ___ H   13. P ___ R

4. h ___ j   9. L ___ N   14. b ___ d

5. K ___ M   10. r ___ t   15. D ___ F

SKILL UNIT NUMBER: RD 451-010.00
WORKSHEET KEY: RD 451-010.12

I. A B C D E F G H I J K L M N O P Q R S T U V W X Y Z

II. a b c d e f g h i j k l m n o p q r s t u v w x y z

III. 1. b   6. X   11. V
      2. f   7. o   12. u
      3. d   8. G   13. Q
      4. l   9. M   14. c
      5. L   10. s   15. E

SKILL UNIT NUMBER: RD 451-010.00
WORKSHEET: Capital and Lower Case Letters: RD 451-010.13

1. Write a capital b _____   10. Write a capital e _____

2. Write a capital q _____   11. Write a capital u _____

3. Write a capital a _____   12. Write a capital h _____

4. Write a capital f _____   13. Write a capital j _____

5. Write a capital l _____   14. Write a capital y _____

6. Write a capital d _____   15. Write a capital t _____

7. Write a capital r _____   16. Write a capital p _____

8. Write a capital g _____   17. Write a capital m _____

9. Write a capital i _____   18. Write a capital n _____

DOCUMENT 10

SKILL UNIT NUMBER: RD 451-010.00
WORKSHEET KEY: RD 451-010.14

1.	B	10.	E
2.	Q	11.	U
3.	A	12.	H
4.	F	13.	J
5.	L	14.	Y
6.	D	15.	T
7.	R	16.	P
8.	G	17.	M
9.	1	18.	N

SKILL UNIT NUMBER: RD 451-010.00
WORKSHEET: RD 451-010.15

1. Write the lower case N. _____   14. Write the lower case J. _____

2. Write the lower case F. _____   15. Write the lower case D. _____

3. Write the lower case S. _____   16. Write the lower case Z. _____

4. Write the lower case 1. _____   17. Write the lower case M. _____

5. Write the lower case W. _____   18. Write the lower case A. _____

6. Write the lower case G. _____   19. Write the lower case K. _____

7. Write the lower case P. _____   20. Write the lower case H. _____

8. Write the lower case T. _____   21. Write the lower case R. _____

9. Write the lower case L. _____   22. Write the lower case B. _____

10. Write the lower case C. _____   23. Write the lower case U. _____

11. Write the lower case Y. _____   24. Write the lower case V. _____

12. Write the lower case Q. _____   25. Write the lower case X. _____

13. Write the lower case O. _____   26. Write the lower case E. _____

SKILL UNIT NUMBER: RD 451-010.00
WORKSHEET KEY: RD 451-010.16

1. n	8. t	15. d	22. b
2. f	9. l	16. z	23. u
3. s	10. c	17. m	24. v
4. i	11. y	18. a	25. x
5. w	12. q	19. k	26. e
6. g	13. o	20. h	
7. p	14. j	21. r	

Instructions: Please look at the letter in column one and then circle
every letter in column two that is the same.   Remember
to circle both the capital and lower case letters for
each one.

I.

1	2
1. a	a c O D Z o A
2. b	L d B i b m C
3. c	P j l C r s c
4. d	g D H t d n o
5. e	E l s L e q u
6. f	V j F z w f v
7. g	G D j g k q J
8. h	o L h H m p t
9. i	P M I o h i T
10. j	B K J l m j c
11. k	D d e f K o k
12. l	L o l H h p m
13. m	n M c C N m q
14. n	s t m N M o n
15. o	p b O T P L o
16. p	O P B p b d L
17. q	Q J f d J q K
18. r	R s T r v W q
19. s	S L P o j s k
20. t	T M l J t v W

1		2						
21.	u	U	M	u	k	L	B	T
22.	v	V	w	R	H	G	v	g
23.	w	W	v	o	n	c	w	M
24.	x	X	x	j	L	l	B	b
25.	y	y	T	t	Y	W	F	f
26.	z	z	Z	j	L	m	o	p

II.

1.	A	A	a	L	B	s	t	o
2.	B	O	D	d	S	B	i	b
3.	C	c	L	D	O	C	o	d
4.	D	D	d	b	B	J	L	l
5.	E	e	F	q	s	f	E	m
6.	F	i	F	g	h	E	f	g
7.	G	Q	p	G	i	q	g	z
8.	H	i	l	J	H	m	o	h
9.	I	H	j	L	I	p	q	i
10.	J	D	d	P	J	q	B	j
11.	K	K	H	l	h	s	k	p
12.	L	m	L	N	l	H	p	q
13.	M	t	M	z	m	s	S	T
14.	N	N	m	M	n	p	H	h
15.	O	O	u	n	o	f	b	z
16.	P	p	i	B	P	b	D	d

17.	Q	q	Q	J	P	p	d	c
18.	R	R	S	T	J	i	l	r
19.	S	L	s	P	S	J	T	A
20.	T	T	A	L	t	l	W	v
21.	U	L	M	U	y	u	W	v
22.	V	V	W	v	J	u	U	j
23.	W	V	u	W	U	B	w	v
24.	X	X	K	T	t	x	k	s
25.	Y	Y	y	u	S	T	U	g
26.	Z	Z	T	z	Y	S	T	l

SKILL UNIT NUMBER: RD 451-010.00
WORKSHEET KEY: RD 451-010.18

Instructions: Please look at the letter in column one and then circle
every letter in column two that is the same. Remember
to circle both the capital and lower case letters for
each one.

I.

1	2
1. a	(a) c O D Z o (A)
2. b	L d (B) l (b) m C
3. c	P j l (C) r s (c)
4. d	g (D) H t (d) n o
5. e	(E) l s L (e) q u
6. f	v j (F) z w (f) v
7. g	(G) D j (g) k q J
8. h	o L (h)(H) m p t
9. i	P M (I) o h (i) T
10. j	B K (J) l m (j) c
11. k	D d e f (K) o (k)
12. l	(L) o (l) H H p m
13. m	n (M) c C N (m) q
14. n	s t m (N) M o (n)
15. o	p b (O) T P L (o)
16. p	O (P) B (p) b d L
17. q	(Q) J f d J (q) K
18. r	(R) s T (r) v W q
19. s	(S) L P o j (s) k
20. t	(T) M l J (t) v W

1	2
21. u	(U) M (u) k L B T
22. v	(V) w R H G (v) g
23. w	(W) v o n c (w) M
24. x	(X) (x) j L l B b
25. y	(y) T t (Y) W F f
26. z	(z) (Z) j L m o p

II.

1	2
1. A	(A) (a) L B s t o
2. B	O D d S (B) i (b)
3. C	(c) L D O (C) o d
4. D	(D) (d) b B J L l
5. E	(e) F q s f (E) m
6. F	i (F) g h E (f) g
7. G	Q p (G) i q (g) z
8. H	i l J (H) m o (h)
9. I	H j L (I) p q (i)
10. J	D d P (J) q B (j)
11. K	(K) H l h s (k) p
12. L	m (L) N (l) H p q
13. M	t (M) z (m) s S T
14. N	(N) m M (n) p H h
15. O	(O) u n (o) f b z
16. P	(p) i B (P) b D d

17. Q   (q) (Q) J   P   p   d   c

18. R   (R) S   T   J   i   l   (r)

19. S   L   (s) P   (S) J   T   A

20. T   (T) A   L   (t) l   W   v

21. U   L   M   (U) y   (u) W   v

22. V   (V) W   (v) J   u   U   j

23. W   V   u   (W) U   B   (w) v

24. X   (X) K   T   t   (x) k   s

25. Y   (Y) (y) u   S   T   U   g

26. Z   (Z) T   (z) Y   S   T   l

SKILL UNIT NUMBER: RD 451-010.00
WORKSHEET: RD 451-010.19

Number each of the following letters in the order which they appear
in the alphabet.

SAMPLE

2	b
5	e
3	c
1	a
4	d

I.

___	d
1	b
___	f
2	c
___	e

II.

___	k
___	h
___	j
___	i
___	l

III.

___	s
___	t
___	v
___	r
___	u

IV.

___	q
___	o
___	n
___	p
___	m

V.

___	v
___	y
___	z
___	w
___	x

VI.

___	V
___	X
___	W
___	Z
___	Y

VII.

___	E
___	G
___	C
___	F
___	D

VIII.

___	H
___	L
___	J
___	K
___	I

IX.

```
_____ T
_____ R
_____ V
_____ S
_____ U
```

X.

```
_____ N
_____ O
_____ Q
_____ P
_____ R
```

XI.

```
_____ B
_____ A
_____ D
_____ C
_____ E
```

SKILL UNIT NUMBER: RD 451-010.00
WORKSHEET KEY: RD 451-010.20

I.

3
1
5
2
4

II.

4
1
3
2
5

III.

2
3
5
1
4

IV.

5
3
2
4
1

V.

1
4
5
2
3

VI.

1
3
2
5
4

VII.

3
5
1
4
2

VIII.

1
5
3
4
2

IX.

3
1
5
2
4

X.

1
2
4
3
5

XI.

2
1
4
3
5

SKILL UNIT NUMBER: RD 451-010.00
WORKSHEET: RD 451-010.21

Number the letters in the order in which they appear in the alphabet.

I.

e _____
x _____
v _____
u _____
b _____
r _____
h _____
k _____
a _____
m _____

II.

c _____
i _____
p _____
t _____
n _____
f _____
s _____
l _____
g _____
w _____

III.

z _____
a _____
x _____
o _____
u _____
r _____
e _____
k _____
f _____
p _____

IV.

o _____
l _____
k _____
p _____
b _____
x _____
c _____
g _____
j _____
h _____

V.

d _____
k _____
v _____
x _____
u _____
w _____
a _____
g _____
m _____
r _____

VI.

s _____
p _____
c _____
e _____
z _____
j _____
r _____
l _____
u _____
a _____

SKILL UNIT NUMBER: RD 451-010.00
WORKSHEET KEY: RD 451-010.22

I.	II.	III.
3	1	10
10	4	1
9	7	9
3	9	5
2	6	8
7	2	7
4	8	2
5	5	4
1	3	3
6	10	6

IV.	V.	VI.
8	2	8
7	4	6
6	8	2
9	10	3
1	7	10
10	9	4
2	1	7
3	3	5
5	5	9
4	6	1

SKILL UNIT NUMBER: RD 451-010.23
ACTIVITY SHEET: RD 451-010.23

Using a teacher made tape, the student will say each letter
of the alphabet as he traces a sandpaper letter with his finger.
In front of the student will be a stack of sandpaper letters
(made by the student) in the order that they occur on the tape.
For example, the directions on the tape will say, "Pick up the
top card. This is the letter 'A.' Say 'A' as you trace the
letter with your finger. This is the letter 'A.' Say 'A.'
Now put the card in the box.

SKILL UNIT NUMBER: RD 451-010.00
ACTIVITY SHEET: RD 451-010.25

I. The student will use clay to form the letters of the
    alphabet missed on the post-test.

II. The student will use his finger to trace letters in a sand
    tray. He will trace only those letters missed on the
    post-test.

6.   Conclusion

The criterion-referenced approach to student diagnosis, placement, and prescription is designed to remove a substantial amount of the guesswork normally required of administrators and teachers in delivering instructional services to students. This is accomplished through detailing the school system's instructional program foundations—the frameworks of skills, concepts, and processes that go into programs. This is followed by the construction of locally tailored criterion-referenced tests. Then, diagnostic and placement documents are developed to provide information on individual and group learning strengths, weaknesses, and areas of questionable skill mastery. Finally, prescription systems are built to afford teachers the mechanism for accessing curricular materials, tests, and auxiliary resources available in the school system's textbooks, workbooks, media, and the prescription systems themselves.

The anticipated results of a criterion-referenced approach are: increased achievement for students; a higher level of sophistication in instructional program delivery; greater teacher and student satisfaction in the teaching/learning process; and a basis for the improvement of programs through the application of findings about students' successes and failures in the process of learning.

The first result is predicated on the notion that students will achieve to a higher degree if they are correctly diagnosed, placed, and prescribed according to a well specified program rather than if none of these functions is performed or if they are haphazardly done in relation to a poorly designed or nonexistant program foundation.

Students do not increase their levels of achievement as a result of a school system's application of some mysterious elixir or the conceptualization of "break-through" programs that will miraculously revolutionize learning. Rather, increasing students' achievement gains occurs as a result of the same type of methodical program design and patient application that medical scientists employed in attacking the causes and cures of polio or cancer. It requires school systems to begin by specifying in writing the foundations for their programs. Next, they ensure that diagnosis and placement against those foundations are correct and lead to accurate prescription and assessment. Finally, they will need to conclude their diagnostic, placement, and prescriptive process by looking at every conceivable thing that goes wrong and cautiously, scientifically, and purposefully take positive steps to improve the process. These changes, in turn, must prove themselves before they become established in the process of program delivery to students.

The second result suggests that school systems will reach a higher level of sophistication in instructional program delivery with a criterion-referenced diagnostic, placement, and prescriptive approach. Many of the woes of classroom teachers are avoidable. Given tools that are even moderately correlated in design, teachers can locate the sources of student learning problems and apply prescriptive activities that are on target. They may not always be able to effect the perfect solution to a student's problem, but they are able to get closer and with some controlled experimentation, find the solution. Ultimately, the teacher cannot do this without the concerted effort of the larger school system committing itself to developing tools and mechanisms for speeding up and increasing the accuracy of the teacher's system of delivery. This means at some point school administrators, teachers, and boards of education will need to recognize that the investment of time, effort, and funds is necessary if the school system is to design the quantity and quality of resources required to facilitate more accurate and sophisticated program delivery.

The third result suggests that teachers and students will find greater satisfaction in the teaching/learning process. The criterion-referenced approach aids teachers in helping students find success in their schooling. If, in fact, students are more accurately diagnosed, placed, and prescribed, they will achieve and feel success. In turn, so will teachers. Further, it would seem that neither the teacher nor the student has been asked to make a sacrifice. The teacher has total option in the teaching process to employ idiosyncratic approaches, as long as these do not cause incorrect student diagnosis, placement, and prescription. The student, on the other hand, is not required to fulfill expectations that are different from those that previously existed in the classroom or programs; only now programs are delivered in a manner that is closely correlated to need, ability, and, hopefully, some degree of student interest.

Finally, the process affords program improvement through the application of findings about students' successes and failures in instructional programs. The process is oriented initially to finding the points at which students can perform successfully in a program. After the issues of correct diagnosis and placement are resolved as factors causing a student's failure, teachers can redirect their attentions to other reasons why failure may be occurring. Is the program logically sequenced? Are the materials appropriate for the students? Why aren't they? Are there other classes of students for whom these materials are also not appropriate? What types of materials are working well with children exhibiting certain learning disabilities? The questions are endless, and they can all be methodically and painstakingly addressed—if the school system and teachers have *first* established that the learning problems evidenced are not a function of inaccurate diagnosis and placement. One could suspect that most school systems have not yet addressed or answered this most critical question: "Are our students correctly diagnosed and placed?" If the question is not answered and resolved in the affirmative, school systems cannot begin to proceed to the more difficult questions posed above. If they attempt to do so anyway, their random efforts will merely be tinkering that will lead to confusion.

A criterion-referenced approach to student diagnosis, placement, and prescription is not a panacea. It does not furnish all of the solutions of educational ills. It does, however, yield a procedure for addressing and attacking problems. This, in turn, will lead to solutions for educational problems that will have a dramatic impact on the success of virtually every type of student enrolled in our school systems.

The following case study is given as a fitting conclusion to the story of Jared Andrews. It is provided to illustrate the integration of the criterion-referenced approach to student diagnosis, placement, and prescription. In addition, the case study depicts that a well-conceived approach to the delivery of prescriptive services can and does result in resolving student learning problems. Whereas the original tale of Jared Andrews was a composite case study and, thereby, fictional, the following study is an accurate accounting of one school system's successful application of student diagnosis, placement, and prescription.

A Case Study

It seemed too early in the school year to have a conference, Mary Jane Andrews had told her husband, Todd. There had to be something wrong. Was Jared already acting up? Or was it going to be another long year of testing, placement, grouping, home study, and conferences all over again? She hoped not.

Todd Andrews had been offered an opportunity to go with another law firm in the adjoining suburban community that summer, and he had accepted the position. Mary Jane could barely contain her enthusiasm for the move, both because of the career opportunity the position change would provide her husband and the prospect of not having to have another conference at Robins Elementary, not having to urge Jared to perform up to the "Robin's standards," and watching her son in a setting of dismal failure. "I'm sure the teachers are as eager to see you move as you are to go," Todd told his wife, "You spent a lot of time at that school. There were times when I wondered who was enrolled at the school—you or Jared," he kidded. But for Mary Jane, it had not been a joking matter. It had been a rough year, and with the move she had hoped that the nightmare was over. Now, it would appear with the call from Jared's new teacher that something was amiss, already.

Only reluctantly had Mary Jane accepted the recommendations of

Miss Johnson and Mr. Edwards that Jared be held back when he transferred from Robins to Adams Elementary. She accepted the logic that it might be in Jared's best interest to repeat the entire third grade even though he had performed fairly well in all of his classes except reading and math. Indeed, it was good fortune that they had moved so that Jared would not have to get adjusted to the idea that he had been retained and face all of the other children with whom he had associated.

Maybe this retention business was not a good idea, she thought, I bet that's the problem. Or, she conjectured, maybe I'm going to get the business about "Adam's standards." At the very least, I hope they set up some plan of action for him and stick to it. The poor kid was in so many groups last year I even lost count, she remembered.

Mary Jane's attitude about the meeting ran from depression to defensiveness as she prepared to drive to the school. She had made up her mind that she would hear the teacher, Miss Morley, out, but she would not give any ground. "I'm not going to go through this again," she told herself aloud. Then, with a sigh of resignation, she realized that there really were no other options. We really can't afford a private school for him, not with the new house and all. And, anyway, what if we put him in a private school and the same thing happened? What would we do then? Finally, shaking her head as if to clear the thoughts away, she told herself, "Just wait for the conference; don't go getting yourself upset." She then proceeded to attack the problem from a different perspective.

Mary Jane was greeted by Miss Morley when she entered the teacher conference room. She was a striking woman, thought Mary Jane. Tall, stately, and nicely shaped. Perhaps, twenty-eight years old.

"It's so nice to see you again, Mrs. Andrews. How have you been?"

"Fine, thank you. But I have to admit I've not looked forward to this meeting—I mean, I've been worried about it," explained Mary Jane.

"Oh, why is that?"

"I just know there is a problem with Jared," she said.

"Well, I did want to sit down with you and visit about Jared ..." said Miss Morley before she was interrupted.

The tears welled up in Mary Jane's eyes, and her voice broke as she related, "I knew that something was wrong. I could just tell, and I don't know what I can do. My husband and I have tried everything."

"Please, Mrs. Andrews. I just want to talk about Jared. He's not having any specific problem. As a matter of fact, he is getting along very well."

"Do you mean you haven't asked me to come because of problems he's having?" queried Mary Jane.

"As a matter of fact, I haven't. The primary purpose is to update you on our diagnostic and placement findings for Jared and to indicate the type of work we have him doing. Finally, we want to enlist your cooperation on a few matters," explained Miss Morley.

Mary Jane looked puzzled. "I don't know that I understand what you are saying. . . . Enlist my cooperation? If there isn't a problem, why do you need my help? And, anyway, how can I help?"

"Maybe it would help us to begin anew, and I'll tell you where we are and what we've done with Jared. Ask me about anything that is unclear. I'm sure that any concerns you have will be eliminated, and it will become obvious the support you can provide us," Miss Morley informed her.

"Fine," said Mary Jane, still uncertain whether or not a problem existed.

"To begin with, at the time we learned that your son had transferred to Adams, during teacher workshop days in late August, we examined the cumulative records that were sent to us by Robins Elementary. When I mention "we," I am referring to the three third grade teachers here at Adams. We examined his files with great detail because of Jared's recommended retention. You see, normally we don't retain students in this school, and we were interested in determining whether or not we felt this recommendation was warranted and desirable."

"You don't retain students? I don't understand. Jared wasn't doing very well at Robins. I considered it very logical that he be retained, even though I was extremely unhappy about it. Though I figured enough wasn't being done for him, he was very far behind," said Mary Jane.

"Let me clear something up. I said that 'normally' we don't retain students. However, there are instances when we do. By and large, however, we don't have to retain students because we individualize and group for instruction at Adams. This simply means that the grade level or classroom in which a student is placed may have no relationship to where he is working in instructional material—a textbook, workbook, or other materials," said Miss Morley.

"I'm lost," exclaimed Mary Jane.

"Well, for example, an eight year old child is normally placed in a third grade classroom. But being placed in a third grade classroom, per se, doesn't mean that he can do third grade work. Some children can't. And other children can. And still other children can do fourth grade work. What we do in Adams is keep the children with their peer group or age group in the same classroom, but if some can only do second grade work, we provide them with second grade skill instruction. Those who are able to do third grade work—most of the students—are instructed on third grade skills, and some who are more advanced get instruction on fourth grade skills. The purpose of keeping the students in the same classroom is to eliminate the child's feeling that he has failed just because he is not doing grade level work," explained Miss Morley.

"In reality, though, isn't the child failing?" asked Mary Jane.

"Not at all. It is normal in most classrooms that *some* children work below grade level, and it is equally normal that some students work above level. Let me give you an illustration. Let's suppose we took all of our third grade children outside and lined them up at the south end of the parking lot. Then we had them race to the north end of the lot. Would you expect all of the children to reach the north end of the lot at the same time?"

"Of course not," said Mary Jane.

"Well, that principle applies totally to a program in a school system. Children are going to vary in their ability to learn, the rate at which they learn, and the level of concepts that they can acquire. This is natural and normal, and the phenomenon will continue throughout their lives. In a sense, I am saying that there is a normal distribution of slow, average, and bright children in the world. The school can help each person learn at his ability, but we cannot make slow children average and average children bright. All we can do is help them learn and progress normally according to the abilities that they have. And this is our job—to make sure that a child *is* learning up to his ability. For some third grade children, working up to ability is working in second grade skills. We can't change this, but we must deal with it," said Miss Morley.

"What happens if you take a fourth grade child, like Jared, who has been retained at third grade and put him back in fourth grade?" asked Mary Jane.

"That all depends. If you put him in fourth grade skills, he will fail. He hasn't learned some of the third grade skills that are necessary as background for fourth grade skills. On the other hand, if he is placed in a fourth grade classroom and instruction centers on the third grade skills he hasn't acquired, the probability of his succeeding is vastly heightened. In fact, that is the recommendation we are making on Jared," stated Miss Morley.

"That sounds beautiful," said Mary Jane.

"I think it's very important that you understand how we arrived at this decision, Mrs. Andrews. And, as I said, we are going to need your help."

"I'd be happy to help in any way that I can," Mary Jane affirmed.

"Good. Let's start again talking about our findings in the cumulative records from Robins. The records were not unlike ones we receive from other school systems. They contained general standardized and diagnostic test results, grades, textbooks completed, and some anecdotal information. They did not include specific references to skill weaknesses Jared has, placement documentation in various subjects, or prescriptions that have been used with him. The standardized and diagnostic test data were of limited value, though they did give us some clues to skills he had not acquired. Also, there were no specific documented reasons for retention other than he wasn't doing well in his classwork, mainly in mathematics and reading. It appeared as though it was recommended that he repeat the entire third grade, all subjects and all skills, as though Jared did not learn anything last year," Miss Morley reported.

"He probably didn't learn anything," Mary Jane quipped.

"That's very unlikely," stated Miss Morley very positively, "but it did cause us to do some testing of our own to fill in a lot of the missing gaps on Jared's background."

"I think you should understand ahead of time that the lack of specificity that we found in Jared's cumulative records is not at all out of the ordinary from the records we receive from other school systems that are transferring students to Adams," said Miss Morley, "and you should not interpret it to mean that the teachers at Robins did not care or were not trying with Jared. Unfortunately, many school systems are less advanced in the specification of their instructional programs, and Robins is an example of that type of school."

"What do you mean?" questioned Mary Jane.

"Well, by and large, it appears that the school system in which Robins is located has not identified those important skills that a child must acquire to demonstrate mastery in its many programs," explained Miss Morley.

"How can you tell?" Mary Jane probed.

"You can tell by the failure of the cumulative record to identify skills with which Jared was having problems; his placement position was cited as a chapter and page number in a book rather than as a skill or concept; the range of diagnostic tests used with Jared indicates that he was tested on the same skills several times which, itself, shows that the teacher was having trouble placing him. There are other signs too, but I don't want to belabor the point. The crucial matter is to illustrate that our ability to locate (diagnose) Jared's problems, establish him in an instructional program (placement), and select and administer correct learning materials (prescription) is dependent upon our understanding of the skills that a child must acquire if he is to learn how to read, for example, with a degree of proficiency," Miss Morley continued.

"You are saying that there are certain skills that a child should acquire if he is to learn to read or do mathematics?" asked Mary Jane.

"That's right. Just like in making a cake, there are certain ingredients that are vital. These must be applied at the right time and in the right amounts. Then, the probability of making a great tasting cake is heightened," reported Miss Morley.

"It sounds simple enough," said Mary Jane.

"It does, but it isn't. I don't want to over-simplify the matter. In fact, the process is very difficult. It requires that a school system first identify the skills, processes, and concepts important in a program. Like this," said Miss Morley as she showed Mrs. Andrews an extract from an instructional program foundation.

"Once the skills have been identified and reaffirmed as crucial to an instructional program," she continued, "we develop a series of tests that assess whether or not a child knows these skills. The tests are developed to measure each one of the skills that are taught in our school system."

"That does sound like work. But why don't you just use tests that are already available . . . you know, the ones companies sell?" Mary Jane asked, "Wouldn't it be simpler?"

"It would be simpler, but it would be less accurate. Unfortunately, commercial tests have a lot of disadvantages, along with their advantages. For example, they test some skills we don't teach; they omit other skills we do teach; they test some skills at grade levels other than where we normally teach those skills; and the directions on who should be administered the tests are too restricted. For example, last year at Robins, Jared was given a standardized test for third grade. He did very poorly in the reading and math sections. He did so poorly, in fact, it was obvious he should never have taken that test, but, rather, a second grade test would have been more appropriate. The second grade test would have shown what he *did* know as well as what he *didn't*. It may have been of some value in placing him. As it turned out, Jared took the third grade test and only proved that he could not do third grade work. That type of information is of no value."

"Why wasn't a second grade test given?" asked Mary Jane.

"Standardized test companies require that each child be administered the test for the grade level in which he is enrolled. Jared was in the third grade, so he took that test. As far as being of diagnostic value—locating Jared's skill problems and where he should be placed—the test results were without value," Miss Morley responded. "These are just a few of the reasons why we design our own tests. We can insure that after the test is administered, we can locate each child's place in our programs and select the instructional materials that should be used with him, immediately," continued Miss Morley.

"How do you do that?" asked Mary Jane.

"I think I can probably show you better than I can explain it. But first, here is a sample copy of the tests we use at Adams. We call them criterion-referenced tests. The title simply means that they, the tests, are developed around our school system's skills," she explained.

Miss Morley continued, "Why don't you put that listing of skills and the test in this folder. You can take them and some other material home with you to share with Mr. Andrews."

"I know he will appreciate that," Mary Jane indicated.

"Now, let's continue. Jared was given the test you have in your folder. The test includes some third and some fourth grade skills. Here is the way he answered the test items. We then had the tests corrected with all of the other tests taken by children in the school, and we received this report, called a diagnostic inventory. As you can see on the individual diagnostic inventory, there are questions or test items for many skills. In fact, there are sixty skills assessed on this test, approximately thirty at the third grade level and the same number at the fourth grade level. Each skill is measured by three items. This means that over a one week period Jared took a 180 item test in reading and a similar test in mathematics. As you look at this inventory, you will notice the pluses and minuses. They indicate how Jared responded to the three items that deal with each skill tested. For example, looking at skill seven, Jared either got all three items wrong on this skill or two items wrong on it. As a consequence, a minus is registered on the inventory that he has probably not mastered the skill. On any skills where Jared got either all three items or two items correct, a plus was registered on the inventory. This indicates he probably has mastered the skill," said Miss Morley.

Mary Jane observed quietly as Miss Morley continued.

"For this particular test, we are attempting to find out (1) Jared's skill strengths and weaknesses and (2) his potential placement position. The pluses and minuses show his probable strengths and weaknesses. We determine his placement position by looking at the statement at the bottom of the sheet which, in Jared's case, says: Skill Placement RD 251-175, Question Number 9, Progressive Tense by Adding -ing. The RD 251-175 is a number for one of the skills that we teach in third grade. The name of the skill follows the number. This skill is where Jared was placed for beginning instruction," explained Miss Morley.

"But how did that statement get on the bottom of the inventory? How was the determination made that that is where Jared should be placed?" asked Mary Jane.

"Each one of our tests has a set of rules that we use to make determinations like this. In the case of this test, our rule is 'at the first point on the test where a student responds incorrectly to any three skills in succession (− − −), the student's placement position is established at the first of the three skills answered successively incorrect.' As you can see, Jared answered skills nine, ten, and eleven incorrectly, as is denoted by three successive minuses. The skill placement position is RD 251-175, Question Number 9."

"What is done about skills four and seven? They have minuses under them, but they come before skill nine. They must not be very important," Mary Jane interjected.

Miss Morley affirmed, "Oh, they are important, and we'll pick them up shortly after instruction is started. But they are not affecting whether or not Jared will do a good job on his placement skill. As I said, the first two things to determine are . . ."

"Jared's strengths and weaknesses and his placement position," Mary Jane interjected with a degree of insight that indicated she was understanding the process.

"That's right. And we've now established those facts," said Miss Morley.

"Now we list other skills with which Jared is having problems— those you've already identified, skills four and seven. We still aren't going to do anything with them, but we do list them and put them in Jared's classroom file for later reference and supplemental instruction."

"The next step is to examine a class grouping report which shows where all of the children in third grade are placed. As you can see, this report shows a series of placement numbers similar to Jared's which, you will recall, is RD 251-175. I've removed the names of the children because this is confidential information, but you can see that there are many different placement positions. We use this report to see how many and which children need to be placed at or near the same skill for beginning instruction. On the basis of this information, we determine how many reading groups we will operate and who will be in them. I'm sure you realized that the purpose of grouping is to get children with similar reading or mathematics strengths working together so that the teacher can be more effective in attending to those children's specific problems," said Miss Morley.

"Yes, I was told that at Robins last year, but I didn't realize the work that teachers go through to accomplish this," said Mary Jane in amazement.

"Well, now we are getting down to the point where we are pre-pared for instruction. We now look at Jared's and his group's place-ment position number, RD 251-175. That number, as I said, corre-sponds to a skill in our reading program. The number also corre-sponds to a skill unit that provides materials and references for teaching that specific skill. For your information, a skill unit looks like this. You may have this. The unit contains worksheets, tests, answer keys, and a wide range of other materials. Most importantly, however, it contains references to books, workbooks, tapes, and other materials that are available in the school that we can use to teach Jared this skill. The exact book and page where the skill is found is stated," exclaimed Miss Morley.

"Do you teach out of these units?" asked Mary Jane.

"By and large, no," said Miss Morley. "We teach out of the textbooks, workbooks, tapes, and other school system materials."

"Why do you need these units then or is that a stupid question," asked Mary Jane shrugging her shoulders.

"No, that's a good question. The greatest value of the units is the time that they save us. They eliminate the guess work in finding where a skill is located in different materials owned by the school system. They speed up the process of placing students. Also, they contain tests that are not available in our books and other mate-rials. And we do use the worksheets and other materials contained in them many times to supplement our basic school system mate-rials. There are a dozen other values like long-range planning assis-tance, guiding volunteer staff, and so forth, but you get the idea," affirmed Miss Morley.

"Yes, I do see the need. Someone could spend a lot of time trying to find the location of skill materials for thirty children without them, couldn't they," said Mary Jane.

"Sometimes a whole year," said Miss Morley. "Going back to Jared's placement position, again, we select the skill unit for skill RD 251-175. We read over portions of it that are vital to give us the flavor of the skill he and his group are on. We then take out one of the unit's back-up tests, and we test him again. I'll anticipate your question, "Why test him again?" We administer a single skill test this time—one that has ten to fifteen items dealing only with skill 251-175. We test to make sure the criterion-referenced test results are correct, that Jared really doesn't know this skill. You see, we expect him to fail the test. If he does, we're okay; if he passes it, then we've got him placed wrong and have to do some further testing. But this doesn't happen very often, and it didn't happen with Jared," explained Miss Morley.

She continued, "Once the back-up test confirmed that Jared was placed correctly, we selected an activity for teaching this skill. As it turned out, we placed him in our basic reading text. After being instructed, with his group, on this skill until we felt he had acquired it, he was tested with another back-up test and demonstrated that the skill was acquired. Since then he has progressed through another five skills without a problem."

"Oh, I'm very pleased to hear that," said Mary Jane.

"You have a right to be. And I'm sure you've seen that Jared is much happier, too," Miss Morley remarked.

"I think he is, but, then, after last year, he has been quite cautious about school. He's not saying much."

"Give him time," suggested Miss Morley, "Now I'd like to share with you some of our thinking about Jared and see what you think."

"Yes, and you can tell me how I can help. I'm very excited about helping out."

Miss Morley began, "You may recall my mentioning that Jared did not appear to have problems in any programs other than reading and mathematics. He is capable of doing fourth grade work in science, social studies, language usage, spelling, handwriting, art, music, health, and physical education. In fact, we've been grouping him with our fourth grade groups since early in the school year. You've also seen that his progress is reading is good, and his work in mathematics is about the same."

"I never dreamed he was making this type of progress," said Mary Jane, unable to control her mounting pleasure.

"Well, our recommendation to you is that we place Jared into Mrs. Byrd's class at fourth grade level. Mrs. Byrd is working with some of the lower level fourth grade students and does a superb job of supplemental instruction in both reading and mathematics. Also, we recommend that Jared continue to be grouped in reading and mathematics with my third grade groups—the ones he's in right now. He's used to those students, and cross grade grouping is very common in Adams. This simply means that during reading and math classes, Jared will leave Mrs. Byrd's class and come to mine for instruction in these subject areas. Mrs. Byrd will follow up my work in her own classroom to strengthen Jared's lessons. If Jared makes substantial improvements, he will be regrouped and receive his reading and mathematics right in Mrs. Byrd's classroom. This is fully what we expect to happen. Do you have any feelings about this?"

"I'm elated! If you think this is the best thing to do, I support you entirely. I'm just so happy that you are finding a solution. And I want you to know that I'll remember your statement about the schools and teachers not being able to remake average students into geniuses. I just want Jared to succeed to the best of his ability."

"I don't think you'll have to worry about that, Mrs. Andrews. Now, there are a few ways you can help us," said Miss Morley.

"Good, anything you say."

"First, I think it's important that you maintain an interest in Jared's school work. Encourage him as he progresses, but realize he is going to have occasional bad days. Don't pressure him for progress reports on school. If he wants to talk with you about school, he will. If he doesn't, he won't. Second, give me a call every couple of weeks for a few months. I'll let you know how things are going and indicate ways you can be of assistance. Third, on occasion, I'll send home some worksheets from our skill units that can be used to reinforce or supplement a skill weakness. I'll tell Jared to work with you on them. You should not do his work, but be available to him if he needs support. Make sure it's quiet in the house when he is studying—no television or radio on. And it would help if you could refrain from watching or listening to television when he is studying, too. He won't feel pressured by 'a good program being on' to hurry his work to be with the family. And, finally, give him all the time he needs. If you can't help him on a particular problem, call me. I'm home most evenings, and I am most willing to help over the phone."

"I'll do everything you say. Is there anything else I should do?" asked Mary Jane.

"Not that I can think of," said Miss Morley. "We'll just proceed as I have outlined it."

"It's been a wonderful conference," said Mary Jane. "I can hardly wait to see Todd and report the good news."

"Well, I'm pleased with your enthusiasm, Mrs. Andrews. I'm sure with your support Jared will do just fine. Thank you so much for coming in."

"Thank you, Miss Morley, I've learned a great deal, and I enjoyed every moment of it."

Miss Morley and Mrs. Andrews left the conference room and walked together to the door. On the way out, Mrs. Byrd was introduced to Mary Jane. After a brief discussion of Jared's move to Mrs. Byrd's class, Mary Jane left the building to meet Todd for dinner. She was more excited about Jared's future than she could ever recall, and Mrs. Byrd's parting statement was one she would remember for years to come, "Don't worry, Jared is going to do just fine."

And he did.

BIBLIOGRAPHY

Block, James H., ed. *Schools, Society, and Mastery Learning*. New York: Holt, Rinehart, and Winston, Inc., 1974.

Bloom, Benjamin, ed. *Taxonomy of Educational Objectives: Handbook I: Cognitive Domain*. New York: David McKay Company, Inc., 1956.

Bruner, Jerome S. *The Process of Education*. Cambridge, Mass.: Harvard University Press, 1960.

Eiss, Albert F. and Harbeck, Mary B. *Behavioral Objectives in the Affective Domain*. Washington, D.C.: National Science Supervisors' Association, 1969.

Johnson, Stuart, R. and Johnson, Rita B. *Developing Individualized Instructional Materials*. New York: Westinghouse Learning Corporation, 1970.

Krathwohl, David R., Bloom, Benjamin S., and Masia, Bertram B. *Taxonomy of Educational Objectives: Handbook II: Affective Domain*. New York: David McKay Company, Inc., 1962.

Mager, Robert F. *Preparing Instructional Objectives*. Palo Alto, Calif.: Fearon Publishers, Inc., 1962.

McAshen, H. H. *Writing Behavioral Objectives: A New Approach*. New York: Harper and Row, Publishers, 1970.

Popham, W. James, ed. *Criterion-Referenced Measurement: An Introduction*. Englewood Cliffs, N.J.: Educational Technology Publications, 1971.

Worner, Roger B. *Designing Curriculum for Educational Accountability: From Continuous Progress Education Through PPBS*. New York: Random House, 1973.

Index